On Conflict

Also by J. Krishnamurti

On Conflict

J. Krishnamurti

HarperSanFrancisco
A Division of HarperCollins*Publishers*

For additional information, write to:
Krishnamurti Foundation Trust, Ltd.
Brockwood Park, Bramdean, Hampshire, England SO24 0LQ

or

Krishnamurti Foundation of America
P.O. Box 1560
Ojai, CA 93024-1560, United States

Sources and acknowledgments can be found on page 137.

Series editor: Mary Cadogan

Associate editors: Ray McCoy and David Skitt

FIRST EDITION

Library of Congress Cataloging-in-Publication Data

Krishnamurti, J. (Jiddu) 1895–1986

    On conflict / J. Krishnamurti. — 1st ed.

    ISBN 0–06–251016–9 (pbk.)

    1. Conduct of life.   2. Interpersonal conflict.   3. Conflict (Psychology)—Philosophy. I. Title.

BJ1595.K75 1994   93–44411

158'.2—dc20   CIP

94 95 96 97 98 99 ❖ CWI 10 9 8 7 6 5 4 3 2 1

This edition is printed on acid-free paper that meets the American National Standards Institute Z39.48 Standard.

The moment you directly question the cause of war, you are questioning your relationship with another, which means that you are questioning your whole existence, your whole way of living.

Bombay, 7 March 1948

You have voluntarily to examine your life, not condemn it, not say this is right or this is wrong but look. When you do look in that way, you will find that you look with eyes that are full of affection—not with condemnation, not with judgment, but with care. You look at yourself with care and therefore with immense affection—and it is only when there is great affection and love that you see the total existence of life.

Madras, 22 December 1965

Contents

Foreword

JIDDU KRISHNAMURTI was born in India in 1895 and, at the age of thirteen, was taken up by the Theosophical Society, which considered him to be the vehicle for the 'world teacher' whose advent it had been proclaiming. Krishnamurti was soon to emerge as a powerful, uncompromising, and unclassifiable teacher, whose talks and writings were not linked to any specific religion and were of neither the East nor the West but for the whole world. Firmly repudiating the messianic image, in 1929 he dramatically dissolved the large and monied organization that had been built around him and declared truth to be 'a pathless land', which could not be approached by any formalized religion, philosophy, or sect.

For the rest of his life Krishnamurti insistently rejected the guru status that others tried to foist upon him. He continued to attract large audiences throughout the world but claimed no authority, wanted no disciples, and spoke always as one individual to another. At the core of his teaching was the realization that fundamental changes in society can be brought about only by a transformation of individual consciousness. The need for self-knowledge and understanding of the restrictive, separative influences of religious and nationalistic conditionings was constantly stressed. Krishnamurti pointed always to the urgent need for openness, for that 'vast space in the brain in which there is unimaginable energy'. This seems to have been the wellspring of his own creativity and the key to his catalytic impact on such a wide variety of people.

Krishnamurti continued to speak all over the world until he died in 1986 at the age of ninety. His talks and dialogues, journals and letters have been preserved in over sixty books and hundreds of recordings. From that vast body of teachings this series of theme books has been compiled. Each book focuses on an issue that has particular relevance to and urgency in our daily lives.

Ojai, 27 May 1945

Questioner: I am sure most of us have seen authentic pictures in movies and magazines of the horrors and barbarities of the concentration camps. What should be done, in your opinion, with those who have perpetrated these monstrous atrocities? Should they not be punished?

Krishnamurti: Who is to punish them? Is not the judge often as guilty as the accused? Each one of us has built up this civilization, has contributed towards its misery, is responsible for its actions. We are the outcome of each other's actions and reactions; this civilization is a collective result. No country or people is separate from another; we are all interrelated; we are one. Whether we acknowledge it or not, when a misfortune happens to a people, we share in it as in its good fortune. You may not separate yourself to condemn or to praise.

   The power to oppress is evil, and every group that is large and well organized becomes a potential source of evil. By shouting about the cruelties of another country, you think you can overlook those of your own. It is not only the vanquished but every country that is responsible for the horrors of war. War is one of the greatest catastrophes; the greatest evil is to kill another. Once you admit such an evil into your heart, you let loose countless minor disasters. You do not condemn war itself but him who is cruel in war.

You are responsible for war; you have brought it about by your everyday action of greed, ill will, passion. Each one of us has built up this competitive, ruthless civilization, in which man is against man. You want to root out the causes of war, of barbarity in others, while you yourself indulge in them. This leads to hypocrisy and to further wars. You have to root out the causes of war, of violence, in yourself, which demands patience and gentleness, not bloody condemnation of others.

Humanity does not need more suffering to make it understand, but what is needed is that you should be aware of your own actions, that you should awaken to your own ignorance and sorrow and so bring about in yourself compassion and tolerance. You should not be concerned with punishment and reward but with the eradication in yourself of those causes that manifest themselves in violence and in hate, in antagonism and ill will. In murdering the murderer, you become like him; you become the criminal. A wrong is not righted through wrong means; only through right means can a right end be accomplished. If you would have peace, you must employ peaceful means, and mass murder, war, can only lead to further murder, further suffering. There can be no love through bloodshed; an army is not an instrument of peace. Only goodwill and compassion can bring peace to the world, not might and cunning nor mere legislation.

You are responsible for the misery and disaster that exist, you who in your daily life are cruel, oppressive, greedy, ambitious. Suffering will continue till you eradicate in yourself those causes that breed passion, greed, and ruthlessness. Have peace and compassion in your heart, and you will find the right answer to your question.

Ojai, 17 June 1945

Questioner: You decry war, and yet are you not supporting it?

Krishnamurti: Are we not all of us maintaining this terrible mass murder? We are responsible, each one, for war; war is an end result of our daily life; it is brought into being through our daily thought-feeling-action. What we are in our occupational, social, religious relationships, that we project; what we are, the world is.

Unless we understand the primary and secondary issues involved in the responsibility for war, we shall be confused and unable to extricate ourselves from its disaster. We must know where to lay the emphasis, and then only shall we understand the problem. The inevitable end of this society is war; it is geared to war; its industrialisation leads to war; its values promote war. Whatever we do within its borders contributes to war. When we buy something, the tax goes towards war; postage stamps help to support war. We cannot escape from war, go where we will, especially now, as society is organized for total war. The most simple and harmless work contributes to war in one way or another. Whether we like it or not, by our very existence we are helping to maintain war. So what are we to do? We cannot withdraw to an island or to a primitive community, for the present culture is everywhere. So what can we do? Shall we refuse to support war by not paying taxes, by not buying stamps? Is that the primary issue? If it is not, and it is only secondary, then do not let us be distracted by it.

Is not the primary issue much deeper, that of the cause of war itself? If we can understand the cause of war, then the secondary issue can be approached from a different point of view altogether; if we do not understand, then we shall be lost in it. If we can free ourselves from the causes of war, then perhaps the secondary problem may not arise at all.

So emphasis must be laid upon the discovery within oneself of the cause of war; this discovery must be made by each one and not by an organized group, for group activities tend to make for thoughtlessness, mere propaganda, and slogans, which only breed further intolerance and strife. The cause must be self-discovered, and thus each one through direct experience liberates himself from it.

If we consider deeply, we are well aware of the causes of war: passion, ill will, and ignorance; sensuality, worldliness, and the craving for personal fame and continuity; greed, envy, and ambition; nationalism with its separate sovereignties, economic frontiers, social divisions, racial prejudices, and organized religion. Cannot each one be aware of his greed, ill will, ignorance, and so free himself from them? We hold to nationalism, for it is an outlet for our cruel, criminal instincts; in the name of our country or ideology we can murder or liquidate with impunity, become heroes, and the more we kill our fellowmen, the more honour we receive from our country.

Now is not liberation from the cause of conflict and sorrow the primary issue? If we do not lay emphasis upon this, how will the solution of the secondary problems stop war? If we do not root out the causes of war in ourselves, of what value is it to tinker with the outward results of our inner state? We must, each one, dig deeply and clear away lust, ill will, and ignorance; we must utterly abandon nationalism, racism, and those causes that breed enmity. We must concern ourselves wholly with that which is of primary importance and not be confused with secondary issues.

Q: You are very depressing. I seek inspiration to carry on. You do not cheer us with words of courage and hope. Is it wrong to seek inspiration?

K: Why do you want to be inspired? Is it not because in yourself you are empty, uncreative, lonely? You want to fill this loneliness, this aching void; you must have tried different ways of filling it, and you hope to escape from it again by coming here. This process of covering up the arid loneliness is called inspiration. Inspiration then becomes a mere stimulation, and, as with all stimulation, it soon brings its own boredom and insensitivity. So we go from one inspiration, stimulation, to another, each bringing its own disappointment and weariness; thus the mind-heart loses its pliability, its sensitivity; the inner capacity of tension is lost through this constant process of stretching and relaxing. Tension is necessary to discover, but a tension that demands relaxation or a stimulation soon loses its capacity to renew itself, to be pliable, alert. This alert pliability cannot be induced from the outside; it comes when it is not dependent upon stimulation, upon inspiration.

Is not all stimulation similar in effect? Whether you take a drink or are stimulated by a picture or an idea, whether you go to a concert or a religious ceremony, or work yourself up over an act, however noble or ignoble, does not all this blunt the mind-heart? A righteous anger, which is an absurdity, however stimulating and inspiring it may be, makes for insensitivity; and is not the highest form of intelligence, sensitivity, receptivity, necessary to experience reality? Stimulation breeds dependence, and dependence, whether worthy or unworthy, causes fear. It is relatively unimportant how one is stimulated or inspired, whether through organized church or politics or through distraction, for the result will be the same—insensitivity caused through fear and dependence.

Distractions become stimulations. Our society primarily encourages distraction, distraction in every form. Our thinking-feeling itself has become a process of wandering away from the centre, from reality. So it is extremely difficult to withdraw from all distractions, for we have become almost incapable of being choicelessly aware of *what is*. So conflict arises, which further distracts our thought-feeling, and it is only through constant awareness that thought-feeling is able to extricate itself from the net of distractions.

Besides, who can give you cheer, courage, and hope? If we rely on another, however great and noble, we are utterly lost, for dependence breeds possessiveness, in which there is endless struggle and pain. Cheer and happiness are not ends in themselves; they are, as courage and hope, incidents in the search of something that is an end in itself. It is this end that must be sought after patiently and diligently, and only through its discovery will our turmoil and pain cease. The journey towards its discovery lies through oneself; every other journey is a distraction leading to ignorance and illusion. The journey within oneself must be undertaken not for a result, not to solve conflict and sorrow; for the search itself is devotion, inspiration. Then the journeying itself is a revealing process, an experience that is constantly liberating and creative. Have you not noticed that inspiration comes when you are not seeking it? It comes when all expectation has ceased, when the mind-heart is still. What is sought after is self-created and so is not the real.

Bombay, 7 March 1948

Questioner: What do you advise us to do if war breaks out?

Krishnamurti: Instead of seeking advice, may I suggest that we examine the problem together? Because it is very easy to advise, but it does not solve the problem. If we examine the problem together, then perhaps we shall be able to see how to act when a war breaks out. It has to be direct action, not action based on somebody else's advice or authority, which would be too stupid in a moment of crisis. In moments of crisis, to follow another leads to our own destruction. After all, in critical times like war, you are led to destruction; but if you know all its implications, see its action, how it comes into being, when the crisis does arise, without seeking advice or following somebody, you will act directly and truly. This does not mean that I am trying to avoid the problem by not answering your question directly. I am not dodging it. On the contrary, I am showing that we can act virtuously—which is not 'righteously'—when this appalling catastrophe comes upon man.

Now, what would you do if there were a war? Being a Hindu, or an Indian, or a German, being nationalistic, patriotic, you would naturally jump to arms, wouldn't you? Because, through propaganda, through horrible pictures, and all the rest of it, you would be stimulated, and you would be ready to fight. Being conditioned by patriotism, nationalism, economic frontiers, by so-called love of country, your immediate response would be to fight. So you would have no problem, would you? You have a problem only when you begin to question the causes of war—which are not merely economic but much more psychological and ideological.

When you begin to question the whole process of war, how war comes into being, then you have to be directly responsible for your actions. Because war comes into being only when you, in your relationship with another, create conflict. After all, war is a projection of our daily life—only more spectacular and more destructive. In daily life we are killing, destroying, maiming thousands through our greed, through our nationalism, through our economic frontiers, and so on. So war is the continuation of your daily existence made more spectacular; and the moment you directly question the cause of war, you are questioning your relationship with another, which means that you are questioning your whole existence, your whole way of living.

If you inquire intelligently, not superficially, when war comes, you will respond according to your inquiry and understanding. A man who is peaceful—not because of an ideal of non-violence, but who is actually free of violence—to him war has no meaning. He will obviously not enter it; he may be shot because he does not, but he accepts the consequences. At least he will not take part in the conflict—but not out of idealism. The idealist is a person who avoids immediate action. The idealist who is seeking non-violence is incapable of being free from violence; because, as our whole life is based on conflict and violence, if I don't understand myself now, today, how can I act truly tomorrow when there is a calamity? Being acquisitive, being conditioned by nationalism, by my class—you know the whole process—how can I, who am conditioned by greed and violence, act without greed and violence when there is a catastrophe? Naturally I will be violent. Also, when there is a war, many people like the bounties of war: the government is going to look after me, to feed my family; and it is a break from my daily routine, from the office, from the monotonous things of life. So war is an escape, and to many it offers an easy way

out of responsibility. Have you heard what many s
'Thank God. It is a beastly business, but at least it
exciting.' Also, war offers a release to our criminal instinct
criminal in our daily life, in our business world, in our relationships, but it is all underground, very carefully hidden, covered over
by a righteous blanket, a legalised acceptance; and war gives us a
release from that hypocrisy—at last we can be violent.

So how you will act in time of war depends upon you,
upon the condition, the state of your being. To say, 'You must not
go to war' to a man who is conditioned to violence is utterly use-
less. It is a waste of time to tell him not to fight, because he is
conditioned to fight, he loves to fight. But those of us who are seriously intentioned can investigate our own lives; we can see how
we are violent in daily life, in our speech, in our thoughts, in our
actions, in our feelings, and we can be free of that violence, not because of an ideal, not by trying to transform it into non-violence,
but by actually facing it, by merely being aware of it; then, when
war comes, we shall be able to act truly. A man who is seeking an
ideal will act falsely, because his response will be based on frus-
tration. Whereas, if we are capable of being aware of our own
thoughts, feelings, and actions in daily life—not condemning them
but just being aware of them—then we will free ourselves from patriotism, from nationalism, from flag-waving, and all that rot, which
are the very symbols of violence; and when we are free, then we
will know how to act truly when that crisis comes that is called war.

Q: Can a man who abhors violence take part in the government of
a country?

K: Now, what is government? After all, it is, it represents, what we
are. In so-called democracy, whatever that may mean, we elect to
represent us those who are like ourselves, those whom we like,
who have got the loudest voice, the cleverest mind, or whatever it
is. So government is what we are, isn't it? And what are we? We are
a mass of conditioned responses—violence, greed, acquisitiveness,

envy, desire for power, and so on. So naturally the government is what we are, which is violence in different forms; and how can a man who really has no violence in his being belong, either in name or in fact, to a structure that is violent? Can reality coexist with violence, which is what we call government? Can a man who is seeking or experiencing reality have anything to do with sovereign governments, with nationalism, an ideology, party politics, a system of power? The peaceful person thinks that by joining the government he will be able to do some good. But what happens when he enters government? The structure is so powerful that he is absorbed by it, and he can do very little. Sir, this is a fact; it is actually happening in the world. When you join a party or stand for election to parliament, you have to accept the party line. So you cease to think. And how can a man who has given himself over to another—whether to a party, a government, or a guru—how can he find reality? And how can he who is seeking truth have any relation to power politics?

You see, we ask these questions because we like to rely on outside authority, on environment, for the transformation of ourselves. We hope leaders, governments, parties, systems, patterns of action will somehow transform us, bring about order and peace in our lives. Surely that is the basis of all these questions, is it not? Can another, be it a government or a guru or a devil, give you peace and order? Can another bring you happiness and love? Surely not. Peace can come into being only when the confusion that we have created is completely understood, not on the verbal level but inwardly; when the causes of confusion, of strife, are removed, obviously there are peace and freedom. But without removing the causes, we look to some outward authority to bring us peace, and the outward is always submerged by the inner. As long as the psychological conflict exists, with its search for power, for position, and so on, however well built, however good and orderly the outward structure may be, the inward confusion always overcomes it. Surely, therefore, we must lay emphasis on the inner and not merely look to the outer.

Bangalore, 11 July 1948

Questioner: How can we solve our present political chaos and the crisis in the world? Is there anything an individual can do to stop war?

Krishnamurti: War is the spectacular and bloody projection of our everyday life. War is merely an outward expression of our inward state, an enlargement of our daily action. It is more spectacular, more bloody, more destructive, but it is the collective result of our individual activities. So you and I are responsible for war, and what can we do to stop it? Obviously, war cannot be stopped by you and me, because it is already in movement; it is already taking place, though still chiefly on the psychological level. It has already begun in the world of ideas, though it may take a little longer for our bodies to be destroyed. As it is already in movement, it cannot be stopped—the issues are too many, too great, and are already committed. But you and I, seeing that the house is on fire, can understand the causes of that fire, can go away from it and build in a new place with different materials that are not combustible, that will not produce other wars. That is all that we can do.

You and I can see what creates wars, and if we are interested in stopping wars, then we can begin to transform ourselves, who are the causes of war. So what causes war, whether religious, political, or economic? Obviously, belief, either in nationalism, an ideology, or a particular dogma. If we had no belief but goodwill,

onsideration between us, then there would be no wars.
e fed on beliefs, ideas, and dogmas, and therefore we
content. The present crisis is of an exceptional nature,
and we as human beings must either pursue the path of constant
conflict and continuous wars that are the result of our everyday action or else see the causes of war and turn our back upon them.

What causes war is the desire for power, position, prestige, money, and also the disease called nationalism, the worship
of a flag, and the disease of organized religion, the worship of a
dogma. All these are the causes of war; and if you as an individual
belong to any of the organized religions, if you are greedy for
power, if you are envious, you are bound to produce a society that
will result in destruction. So again, it depends upon you and not
on the leaders, not on Stalin, Churchill, and all the rest of them. It
depends upon you and me, but we do not seem to realize that. If
once we really felt the responsibility of our own actions, how
quickly we could bring to an end all these wars, this appalling
misery! But, you see, we are indifferent. We have three meals a
day, we have our jobs, we have our bank accounts, big or little,
and we say, 'For God's sake, don't disturb us, leave us alone'. The
higher up we are, the more we want security, permanency, tran-
quillity, the more we want to be left alone, to maintain things
fixed as they are; but they cannot be maintained as they are, because there is nothing to maintain. Everything is disintegrating.
We do not want to face these things; we do not want to face the
fact that you and I are responsible for wars. You and I may talk
about peace, have conferences, sit around a table, and discuss; but
inwardly, psychologically, we want power, position; we are moti-
vated by greed. We intrigue, we are nationalistic, we are bound by
beliefs, by dogmas, for which we are willing to die and destroy
each other. Do you think such men, you and I, can have peace in
the world? To have peace, we must be peaceful. To live peacefully means not to create antagonism. Peace is not an ideal. To
me, an ideal is merely an escape, an avoidance, a contradiction of
what is. An ideal prevents direct action upon what is. But to have

peace, we will have to love, we will have to begin, not to live an ideal life, but to see things as they are and act upon them, transform them. As long as each one of us is seeking psychological security, the physiological security we need—food, clothing, and shelter—is destroyed. We are seeking psychological security, which does not exist; and we seek it, if we can, through power, through position, through titles, names—all of which are destroying physical security. This is an obvious fact, if you look at it.

So to bring about peace in the world, to stop all wars, there must be a revolution in the individual, in you and me. Economic revolution without this inward revolution is meaningless, for hunger is the result of the maladjustment of economic conditions produced by our psychological states—greed, envy, ill will, and possessiveness. To put an end to sorrow, to hunger, to war, there must be a psychological revolution, and few of us are willing to face that. We will discuss peace, plan legislation, create new leagues, the United Nations, and so on; but we will not win peace, because we will not give up our position, authority, money, property, our stupid lives. To rely on others is utterly futile; others cannot bring us peace. No leader is going to give us peace, no government, no army, no country. What will bring peace is inward transformation that will lead to outward action. Inward transformation is not isolation, is not a withdrawal from outward action. On the contrary, there can be right thinking, but there is no right thinking when there is no self-knowledge. Without knowing yourself, there is no peace.

To put an end to outward war, you must begin to put an end to war in yourself. Some of you will shake your heads and say, 'I agree', and go outside and do exactly the same as you have been doing for the last ten or twenty years. Your agreement is merely verbal and has no significance, for the world's miseries and wars are not going to be stopped by your casual assent. They will be stopped only when you realize the danger, when you realize your responsibility, when you do not leave it to somebody else. If you see the suffering, if you see the urgency of immediate action and do not postpone it, then you will transform yourself; and peace will come only when you yourself are peaceful, are at peace with your neighbour.

Q: The family is the framework of our love and greed, of our selfishness and division. What is its place in your scheme of things?

K: I have no scheme of things. See how absurdly we think of life! Life is living, dynamic, active, and you cannot put it in a frame. It is the intellectuals who put life in a frame, who have a scheme to systematise it. I have no scheme, but let us look at the facts. First, there is the fact of our relationship with another, whether it is with a wife, a husband, or a child—the relationship that we call the family. Let us examine the fact of what is, not what we should like it to be. Anyone can have ideas about family life; but if we can look at, examine, understand what is, then perhaps we shall be able to transform it. But merely to cover up what is with a lovely set of words—calling it responsibility, duty, love—all that has no meaning. So let us examine what we call the family. To understand something, we must examine what is and not cover it up with sweet-sounding phrases.

What is it that you call the family? Obviously, it is a relationship of intimacy, of communion. Now, in your family, in your relationship with your wife, with your husband, is there communion? Surely that is what we mean by relationship. Relationship means communion without fear, freedom to understand each other, to communicate directly. Obviously, relationship means that—to be in communion with another. Are you? Are you in communion with your wife? Perhaps you are physically, but that is not relationship. You and your wife live on opposite sides of a wall of isolation, do you not? You have your own pursuits, your ambitions, and she has hers. You live behind the wall and occasionally look over the top, and that you call relationship. You may enlarge it, soften it, introduce a new set of words to describe it, but that is the actual fact—that you and another live in isolation, and that life in isolation you call relationship.

Now, if there is real relationship between two people, which means there is communion between them, then the implications are enormous. Then there is no isolation, then there is love and not responsibility or duty. It is people who are isolated behind their walls who talk about duty and responsibility. But a man who loves does not talk about responsibility—he loves. Therefore he shares with another his joy, his sorrow, his money. Are our families such? Is there direct communion with your wife, with your children? Obviously not. Therefore the family is merely an excuse to continue your name or tradition, to give you what you want, sexually or psychologically. The family becomes a means of self-perpetuation. That is one kind of immortality, one kind of permanency. Also, the family is used as a means of gratification. I exploit others ruthlessly in the business world, in the political or social world outside, and at home I try to be kind and generous. How absurd! Or the world is too much for me; I want peace, and I go home. I suffer in the world, and I go home and try to find comfort. So I use relationship as a means of gratification, which means I do not want any disturbance of it.

In our families there is isolation and not communion, and therefore no love. Love and sex are two different things, which we will discuss another time. We may develop in our isolation a form of selflessness, a devotion, a kindness, but it is always behind the wall, because we are more concerned with ourselves than with others. If you were concerned with others, if you were really in communion with your wife or your husband, and were therefore open to your neighbour, the world would not be in this misery. That is why families in isolation become a danger to society.

So how can this isolation be broken down? To do that, we must be aware of it; we must not be detached from it or say that it does not exist. It does exist; that is an obvious fact. Be aware of the way you treat your wife, your husband, your children; be aware of the callousness, the brutality, the traditional assertions, the false education. Do you mean to say that if you loved your wife or your husband, we would have this conflict and misery in the world? It is because you do not know how to love your wife, your husband, that you don't know how to love God. You want God as a further means of isolation, a further means of security. After all, God is the ultimate security; but such a search is not for God, it is merely a refuge, an escape. To find God you must know how to love, not God, but the human beings around you, the trees, the flowers, the birds. Then, when you know how to love them, you will really know what it is to love God. Without loving another, without knowing what it means to be completely in communion with one another, you cannot be in communion with truth. But you see, we are not thinking of love; we are not concerned with being in communion with another. We want security, either in the family, in property, or in ideas; and where the mind is seeking security, it can never know love. For love is the most dangerous thing, because when we love somebody, we are vulnerable, we are open; and we do not want to be open and vulnerable. We want to be enclosed, to be more at ease within ourselves.

To bring about transformation in our relationship is not a matter of legislation, of compulsion according to scripture. To bring about radical transformation in relationship, we must begin with ourselves. Watch yourself, how you treat your wife and children. Your wife is a woman, and that is the end of it—she is to be used as a doormat! I don't think you realize what a catastrophic state the world is in at the present time; otherwise you wouldn't be so casual about all this. We are at the edge of a precipice—moral, social, and spiritual. You don't see that the house is burning and you are living in it. If you knew that the house was burning, that you were on the edge of a precipice, you would act. But unfortunately you are complacent, afraid, comfortable; you are dull or weary, demanding immediate satisfaction. You let things drift, and therefore the world's catastrophe is approaching. It is not a mere threat; it is an actual fact. In Europe war is already moving—war, war, war, disintegration, insecurity. After all, what affects another affects you. You are responsible for another, and you cannot shut your eyes and say, 'I am secure in Bangalore'. That is obviously a very short-sighted and stupid thought.

The family becomes a danger where there is isolation between husband and wife, between parents and children, because then the family encourages general isolation; but when the walls of isolation are broken down in the family, then you are in communion not only with your wife and children but with your neighbour. Then the family is not enclosed, limited; it is not a refuge, an escape. So the problem is not somebody else's but our own.

Poona, 1 September 1948

Questioner: In view of war and the possible atomic devastation of humanity, is it not futile to concentrate on mere individual transformation?

Krishnamurti: This is a very complicated question and needs very careful study. I hope you will have the patience to go step by step with me and not leave off halfway. The causes of war are fairly obvious, and even a schoolboy can see them—greed, nationalism, the search for power, geographical and national divisions, economic conflicts, sovereign states, patriotism, one ideology, whether of the left or right, trying to impose itself upon another, and so on. These causes are created by you and me. War is the spectacular expression of our daily existence. We identify ourselves with a particular group, national, religious, or racial, because it gives us a sense of power, and power inevitably brings about catastrophe. You and I are responsible for war, not Hitler, Stalin, or some other superleader. It is convenient to say that capitalists or insane leaders are responsible for war. At heart, each one wants to be wealthy; each one wants power. These are the causes of war, for which you and I are responsible.

  I think it is fairly clear that war is the result of our daily existence, only more spectacularly, more bloodily so. Since we are all trying to accumulate possessions, pile up money, naturally we create a society with frontiers, boundaries, and tariff walls; and when one isolated nationality comes into conflict with another, inevitably war results—that is a fact. I do not know if you have thought of this problem at all. We are confronted with war, and must we not find who is responsible for it? Surely, a sane man will see that he is responsible and will say, 'Look, I am creating this war. Therefore I shall cease to be national. I shall have no patriotism, no nationality. I shall not be Hindu, Moslem, or Christian but a human being.' That requires a certain clarity of thought and perception, which most of us are unwilling to face. If you personally are opposed to war—but not for the sake of an ideal, because ideals are an impediment to direct action—what are you to do? What is a sane man to do who is opposed to war? First, he must cleanse his own mind, free himself from the causes of war, such as greed. Therefore since you are responsible for war, it is important to free yourself from its causes. That means, among other things, that you must cease to be national. Are you willing to do that? Obviously not, because you like to be called a Hindu, a brahmin, or whatever your label is. That means that you worship the label and prefer it to living sanely and rationally; so you are going to be destroyed, whether you like it or not.

What is a person to do if he wants to free himself from the causes of war? How is he to stop war? The momentum of greed, the power of nationalism, which every human being has set in motion—can they be stopped? Obviously they cannot. War can be stopped only when Russia, America, and all of us transform ourselves immediately and say that we will have no nationalism; we will not be Russians, Americans, Hindus, Moslems, Germans, or Englishmen, but human beings; we will be human beings in relationship, trying to live happily together. If the causes of war are eradicated from the heart and mind, then there is no war. But the momentum of power is still going on. I will give you an example. If a house is burning, what do we do? We try to save as much of the house as possible, and then we study the causes of the fire. We find the right kind of brick, the proper fire-resisting material, improved construction, and so on, and we build anew. In other words, we leave the house that is burning. Similarly, when a civilization is crumbling, is destroying itself, sane men who see they cannot do anything about it build a new one that will not burn. Surely, that is the only way to act, that is the only rational method—not merely to reform the old, to patch up the burning house.

Now, if I were to collect together, at this meeting and elsewhere, all who feel they are really free from the causes of war, what would happen? That is, can peace be organized? Look at the implications of it, see what is involved in organizing peace. One of the causes of war is the desire for power—individual, group, and national. What happens if we form an organization for peace? We become a focal point of power, and the pursuit of power is one of the causes of war. The moment we organize for peace, we inevitably invite power; and when we have power, we are again creating the causes of war. So what am I to do? Seeing that one of the causes of war is power, am I to oppose war, which means further power? In the very process of opposition, am I not creating power? Therefore my problem is quite different. It is not an organizational problem. I cannot talk to a group, but only to you as an individual, showing you the causes of war. You and I as individuals must give our thought to it and not leave it to somebody else. Surely, as in a family, when there is affection, when there is mercy, we need no organization for peace. What we need is mutual understanding, mutual cooperation. When there is no love, inevitably there is war.

To understand the complex problem of war, one must approach it very simply. To approach it simply is to understand one's own relationship to the world. If in that relationship there is a sense of power, a sense of domination, that relationship inevitably creates a society based on power, on domination, which in turn brings about war. I may see that very clearly, but if I tell ten people about it and organize them, what have I done? I have created power, have I not? No organization is necessary. The organization is the power element that brings about war. There must be individuals who are opposed to war; but when you gather them into an organization or represent a creed, you are in the same position as the warmonger. Most of us are satisfied with words, we live on words without meaning, but if we examine the problem very closely, very clearly, then the problem itself yields the answer. You do not have to seek it. So each one of us must be aware of the causes of war, and each one must be free of them.

Q: Instead of having hair-splitting discussions on such a question as being and becoming, why do you not apply yourself to some of the burning questions of the country and show us a way out? What is your position, for instance, on the questions of Hindu-Moslem unity, Pakistan-India amity, brahmin and non-brahmin rivalry? You will do a great service if you can suggest an effective solution to these difficult problems.

K: Whether there should be unity among Hindus and Moslems is a problem like those that human beings throughout the world are having. Are they difficult problems—or are they childish, immature problems? Surely, we ought to have outgrown this childish kind of business, and do you call these the burning problems of the day? When you call yourself a Hindu and say you belong to a particular religion, are you not quarrelling over words? What do you mean by Hinduism? A group of beliefs, dogmas, traditions, and superstitions. Is religion a matter of belief? Surely, religion is the search for truth, and religious people are not those who have these stupid ideas. The man who is searching for truth is a religious man, and he has no need for labels—Hindu, Moslem, or Christian. Why do we call ourselves these names? Because we are not really religious people at all. If we had love, mercy in our hearts, we would not care two pins what we called ourselves— and that *is* religion. It is because our hearts are empty that they are filled with things that are childish—and which you call the burning questions! Surely, that is very immature. Whether there should be brahmins and non-brahmins—are these the burning problems, or are they a front behind which you are hiding? After all, who is a brahmin? Surely, not he who wears the sacred thread. A brahmin is a person who understands, who has no authority in society, is independent of society, is not greedy, is not seeking power, is outside all power—such a person is a brahmin. Are you and I such people? Obviously we are not. Then why call ourselves by a label that has no meaning? You call yourself by that label because it is profitable; it gives you a position in society. A sane man does not belong to any group; he does not seek position in a society, which only breeds war. If you were really sane, it would not matter what you are called; you would not worship a label. But labels, words, become important when the heart is empty. Because your heart is empty, you are frightened and are willing to kill others. It is really an absurd problem, this matter of Hindus and Moslems. When you see immature people making a mess of things, what do you do? It is no use hitting them on the head. Either you try to help them, or you withdraw and leave them entirely free to make their mess. They like their toys, so you withdraw and build a new culture, a new society. Nationalism is a poison, patriotism is a drug, and the world conflicts are a distraction from direct relationship with people. If you know that, can you indulge in them anymore? If you see that clearly, there will be no division between Hindu and Moslem. Our problem then is much vaster, and we will not therefore lose ourselves in stupid problems in the face of the real issues of life.

These real issues are near at hand, in the battle between you and me, between husband and wife, between you and your neighbour. Out of our personal lives we have created this mess, these quarrels between brahmin and non-brahmin, between Hindu and Moslem. You and I have contributed to this mess, and we are directly responsible, not some leaders. Since it is our responsibility, we have to act; and to act, we must think rightly; and to think rightly, we have to put away childish things, all that we know to be utterly false and without meaning. To be mature human beings, we must put away the absurd toys of nationalism, of organized religion, of following somebody politically or religiously. That is our problem. If you are really earnest, serious about all this, then you will naturally free yourself from infantile acts, from calling yourself by particular labels, whether national, political, or religious; and only then shall we have a peaceful world. But if you merely listen, you will go out and do exactly the same thing that you have done before. I know you laugh—and that is where the tragedy lies. You are not interested in stopping war; you are not really interested in having peace in the world.

We are all on the brink of a precipice. This whole civilization that man has believed in may be destroyed; the things that we have produced, tenderly cultivated—everything is now at stake. For man to save himself from the precipice, there must be a real revolution—not a bloody revolution but a revolution of inward regeneration. There cannot be regeneration without self-knowledge. Without knowing yourself, there is nothing you can do. We have to think out every problem anew; and to do that, we must free ourselves from the past, which means that the thought process must come to an end. Our problem is to understand the present in its enormity with its inevitable catastrophes and miseries—we must face it all anew. There can be no newness if we merely carry on with the past, if we analyse the present through the thought process. That is why, to understand a problem, the thought process must cease. When the mind is still, quiet, tranquil—only then is the problem resolved. Therefore it is important to understand oneself. You and I must be the salt of the earth, professing a new thought, a new happiness.

Bombay, 19 February 1950

Questioner: Through such movements as the United Nations and the World Pacifist Conferences, men all over the world are making an individual and collective effort to prevent a third world war. How does your attempt differ from theirs, and do you hope to have any appreciable results? Can war be prevented?

Krishnamurti: Let us first dispose of the obvious facts and then go more deeply into the matter. Can we prevent war? What do you think? Men are bent on slaughtering each other; you are bent on slaughtering your neighbour—not with swords, perhaps, but you are exploiting them, politically, religiously, and economically. There are social, communal, linguistic divisions, and are you not making a great ado about all this? You do not want to prevent war because some of you are going to make money. The cunning are going to make money, and the stupid also will want to make more. For God's sake, see the ugliness, the ruthlessness of it! When you have a set purpose of gain at all costs, the result is inevitable. The third world war arises from the second world war, the second world war arose from the first, and the first was the result of previous wars. Until you put an end to the cause, mere tinkering with the symptoms has no significance. One of the causes of war is nationalism, sovereign governments, and all the ugliness that goes with them—power, prestige, position, and authority. But most of us do not want to put an end to war because our lives are incomplete, our whole existence is a battlefield, a ceaseless conflict, not only with one's wife, one's husband, one's neighbour but with ourselves—the constant struggle to become something. That is our life, of which war and the hydrogen bomb are merely the violent and spectacular projections. As long as we do not understand the whole significance of our existence and bring about a radical transformation, there can be no peace in the world.

Now the second problem is much more difficult, much more demanding of your attention—which does not mean that the first one is not important. It is that most of us pay scant attention to the transformation of ourselves because we do not *want* to be transformed. We are contented and do not want to be disturbed. We are satisfied to go along as we are, and that is why we are sending our children to war, why we must have military training. You all want to save your bank accounts, hold on to your property—all in the name of non-violence, in the name of God and peace, which is a lot of sanctimonious nonsense. What do we mean by peace? You say the United Nations is trying to establish peace by organizing its member nations, which means it is balancing power. Is that the pursuit of peace?

Then there is the gathering of individuals around a certain idea of what they consider to be peace. That is, the individual resists war according to either his moral persuasion or his economic ideas. We place peace either on a rational basis or on a moral basis. We say we must have peace because war is not profitable, which is the economic reason; or we say we must have peace because it is immoral to kill, it is irreligious, man is godly in his nature and must not be destroyed, and so on. So there are all these explanations of why we should not have war; the religious, moral, humanitarian, or ethical reasons for peace on the one hand and the rational, economic, or social reasons on the other.

Now, is peace a thing of the mind? If you have a reason, a motive for peace, will that bring about peace? If I refrain from killing you because I think it is immoral, is that peaceful? If for economic reasons I do not join the army because I think it is unprofitable, is that peaceful? If I base my peace on a motive, on a reason, can that bring about peace? If I love you because you are beautiful, because you please me bodily, is that love? This is very important. Most of us have so cultivated our minds, we are so intellectual, that we want to find reasons for not killing, the reasons being the appalling destructiveness of the atomic bomb, the moral and economic arguments for peace, and so on; and we think that the more reasons we have for not killing, the more there will be peace. But can you have peace through a reason? Can peace be made into a cause? Is not the very cause part of the conflict? Is non-violence, is peace an ideal to be pursued and attained eventually through a gradual process of evolution? These are all reasons, rationalizations, are they not?

So if we are at all thoughtful, our question really is whether peace is a result, the outcome of a cause, or whether peace is a state of being, not in the future or in the past but now. If peace, if non-violence is an ideal, surely it indicates that actually you are violent; you are not peaceful. You *wish* to be peaceful, and you give reasons why you *should* be peaceful; and, being satisfied with the reasons, you remain violent. Actually, a man who wants peace, who sees the necessity of being peaceful, has no ideal about peace. He does not make an effort to become peaceful but sees the necessity, the truth of being peaceful. It is only the man who does not see the importance, the necessity, the truth of being peaceful, who makes non-violence an ideal—which is really only a postponement of peace. That is what you are doing: you are all worshipping the ideal of peace and in the meantime enjoying violence. You laugh; you are easily amused. It is another entertainment; and when you leave this meeting, you will go on exactly as before! Do you expect to have peace by facile arguments and casual talk? You will not have peace because you do not want peace; you are not interested in it; you do not see the importance, the necessity of having peace now, not tomorrow. It is only when you have no reason for being peaceful that you will have peace.

As long as you have a reason to live, you are not living, are you? You live only when there is no reason, no cause—you just live. Similarly, as long as you have a reason for peace, you will have no peace. A mind that invents a reason for being peaceful is in conflict, and such a mind will produce chaos and conflict in the world. Just think it out, and you will see. How can the mind that invents reasons for peace be peaceful? You can have very clever arguments and counter-arguments, but is not the very structure of the mind based on violence? The mind is the outcome of time, of yesterday, and it is always in conflict with the present; but the man who really wants to be peaceful now has no reason for it. For the peaceful man, there is no motive for peace. Has generosity a motive? When you are generous with a motive, is that generosity? When a man renounces the world in order to achieve God, in order to find something greater, is that renunciation? If I give up this in order to find that, have I really given up anything? If I am peaceful for various reasons, have I found peace?

So then, is not peace a thing far beyond the mind and the inventions of the mind? Most of us, most religious people with their organizations, come to peace through reason, through discipline, through conformity, because there is no direct perception of the necessity, the truth of being peaceful. Peacefulness, that state of peace, is not stagnation; on the contrary, it is a most active state. But the mind can only know the activity of its own creation, which is thought; and thought can never be peaceful; thought is sorrow; thought is conflict. As we know only sorrow and misery, we try to find ways and means to go beyond it, and whatever the mind invents only further increases its own misery, its own conflict, its own strife. You will say that very few will understand this, that very few will ever be peaceful in the right sense of the word. Why do you say that? Is it not because it is a convenient escape for you? You say that peace can never be achieved in the way I am talking about; it is impossible. Therefore you must have reasons for peace; you must have organizations for peace; you must have clever propaganda for peace. But all those methods are obviously mere postponement of peace.

Only when you are directly in touch with the problem, when you see that without peace today you cannot have peace tomorrow, when you have no reason for peace but actually see the truth that without peace life is not possible, creation is not possible, that without peace there can be no sense of happiness—only when you see the truth of that will you have peace. Then you will have peace without any organizations for peace. For that you must be so vulnerable, you must demand peace with all your heart, you must find the truth of it for yourself, not through organizations, through propaganda, through clever arguments for peace and against war. Peace is not the denial of war. Peace is a state of being in which all conflicts and all problems have ceased; it is not a theory, not an ideal to be achieved after ten incarnations, ten years, or ten days. As long as the mind has not understood its own activity, it will create more misery; and the understanding of the mind is the beginning of peace.

Talk to Students at Rajghat School, 22 January 1954

Questioner: What is conflict, and how does it arise in our mind?

Krishnamurti: You want to be the captain of a cricket team. But there is somebody else better than you. You do not like that. So you have a conflict. You want to get something, you cannot, and so there is conflict. If you can get what you want, then the difficulty is to keep it; so you struggle again or want more of it. So there is always a conflict going on because you always want something. If you are a clerk, you want to become a manager; if you have a cycle, you want a motor car, and so on; if you are miserable, you want to be happy.

So what you want is not important, but what you *are* is. The understanding of what you are, going into it, seeing all the implications of what you are—that frees you from conflict.

Rajghat, 9 January 1955

Questioner: What about the atomic and the hydrogen bombs? Can we discuss that?

Krishnamurti: That involves the whole problem of war and how to prevent it. Can we discuss that so as to clarify our own minds, pursue it seriously, earnestly, to the end and thereby know the truth of the matter completely?

What do we mean by peace? Is peace the opposite, the antithesis of war? If there were no war, would we have peace? Are we pursuing peace, or is what we call peace merely a space between two contradictory activities? Do we really want peace, not only at one level, economic or spiritual, but totally? Or is it that we are continually at war within ourselves and therefore outwardly? If we wish to prevent war, we must obviously take certain steps, which really means having no frontiers of the mind, because belief creates enmity. If you believe in communism and I believe in capitalism, or if you are a Hindu and I am a Christian, obviously there is antagonism between us. So if you and I desire peace, must we not abolish all these frontiers of the mind? Or do we merely want peace in terms of satisfaction, maintaining the status quo after achieving a certain result?

You see, I don't think it is possible for individuals to stop war. War is like a giant mechanism that, having been set going, gathers great momentum, and probably it will go on and we shall be crushed, destroyed in the process. But if one wishes to step out of that mechanism, the whole machinery of war, what is one to do? That is the problem. Do we really want to stop war, inwardly as well as outwardly? After all, war is merely the dramatic outward expression of our inward struggle, is it not? And can each one of us cease to be ambitious? Because as long as we are ambitious, we are ruthless, which inevitably produces conflict between ourselves and others as well as between one group or nation and another. This means, really, that as long as you and I are seeking power in any direction, power being evil, we must produce wars. And is it possible for each of us to investigate the process of ambition, of competition, of wanting to be somebody in the field of power, and to put an end to it? It seems to me that only then can we as individuals step out of this culture, this civilization that is producing wars.

Can we as individuals put an end in ourselves to the causes of war? One of the causes is obviously belief, the division of ourselves as Hindus, Buddhists, Christians, communists, or capitalists. Can we put all that aside?

Q: All the problems of life are unreal, and there must be something real on which we can rely. What is that reality?

K: Do you think the real and the unreal can so easily be divided? Or does the real come into being only when I begin to understand what is unreal? Have you even considered what the unreal is? Is pain unreal? Is death unreal? If you lose your bank account, is that unreal? A man who says, 'All this is unreal, therefore let us find the real', is escaping from reality.

Can you and I put an end in ourselves to the factors that contribute to war within and without? Let us discuss that, not merely verbally but really investigate it, go into it earnestly and see if we can eradicate in ourselves the cause of hate, of enmity, this sense of superiority, ambition, and all the rest of it. Can we eradicate all this? If we really want peace, it must be eradicated. If you would find out what is real, what is God, what is truth, you must have a very quiet mind; and can you have such a mind if you are ambitious, envious, if you are greedy for power, position, and all that? Does not seriousness consist in understanding the process of the mind, of the self, which creates all these problems, and dissolving it?

Q: How can we uncondition ourselves?

K: But I am showing you! What is conditioning? It is the tradition that has been imposed upon you from childhood and the beliefs, the experiences, the knowledge that one has accumulated for oneself. They are all conditioning the mind.

Now, before we go into the more complex aspects of the question, can you cease to be a Hindu, with all its implications, so that your mind is capable of thinking, responding, not according to a modified Hinduism but completely anew? Can there be in you a total revolution so that the mind is fresh, clear, and therefore capable of investigation? That is a very simple question. I can give a talk about it, but it will have no meaning if you merely listen and then go away agreeing or disagreeing, whereas if you and I can discuss this problem and go through it together to the very end, then perhaps our talking will be worthwhile. So can you and I, who wish to have peace, or who talk about peace, eradicate in ourselves the causes of antagonism, of war?

Q: Are individuals impotent against the atomic and hydrogen bombs?

K: They are going on experimenting with these bombs in America, Russia, and elsewhere, and what can you and I do about it? So what is the point of discussing this matter? You may try to create public opinion by writing to the papers about how terrible it is, but will that stop governments from investigating and creating the H-bomb? They may use atomic energy for peaceful as well as destructive purposes, and probably within five or ten years they will have factories running on atomic energy; but they will also be preparing for war. They may limit the use of atomic weapons, but the momentum of war is there, and what can we do? Historical events are in movement, and I don't think you and I living here can stop that movement. But what we can do is something completely different. We can step out of the present machinery of society, which is constantly preparing for war, and perhaps by our own total inward revolution we shall be able to contribute to the building of a civilization that is altogether new.

After all, what is civilization? What is the Indian or the European civilization? It is an expression of the collective will, is it not? The will of the many has created this present civilization in India, and cannot you and I break away from it and think entirely differently about these matters? Is it not the responsibility of serious people to do this? Must there not be people who see this process of destruction going on in the world, who investigate it, and who step out of it in the sense of not being ambitious and all the rest of it? What else can we do? But you see, we are not willing to be serious; that is the difficulty. We don't want to tackle ourselves; we want to discuss something outside, far away.

Q: There must be some people who are very serious, and have they solved their problems or the problems of the world?

K: That is not a serious question, is it? It is like my saying that others have eaten when I myself am hungry. If I am hungry, I will inquire where food is to be had, and to say that others are well fed is irrelevant. It indicates that I am not really hungry. Whether there are serious people who have solved their problems is not important. Have you and I solved *our* problems? That is much more important. Can a few of us discuss this matter very seriously, earnestly pursue it and see what we can do, not merely intellectually, verbally, but actually?

Q: Is it really possible for us to escape the impact of modern civilization?

K: What is modern civilization? Here in India it is an ancient culture on which have been superimposed certain layers of Western culture like nationalism, science, parliamentarianism, militarism, and so on. Now, either we shall be absorbed by this civilization, or we must break away and create a different civilization altogether.

It is an unfortunate thing that we are so eager merely to listen, because we listen in the most superficial manner, and that seems to be sufficient for most of us. Why does it seem so extraordinarily difficult for us seriously to discuss and eradicate in ourselves the things that are causing antagonism and war?

Q: We have to consider immediate problems.

K: In considering the immediate problem, you will find that it has deep roots; it is the result of causes that lie within ourselves. So to resolve the immediate problem, should you not investigate the deeper problems?

Q: There is only one problem, and that is to find out what is the end of life.

K: Can we discuss that really seriously, go into it completely, so that we know for ourselves what is the end of life? What is life all about? Where is it leading? That is the question, not what is the purpose of life. If we merely seek a definition of the purpose of life, you will define it in one way and I in another, and we shall wrongly choose what we think is the better definition according to our idiosyncrasies. Surely that is not what the questioner means. He wants to know what is the end of all this struggle, this search, this constant battle, this coming together and parting, birth and death. What is the whole of existence leading to? What does it mean?

Now, what is this thing that we call life? We know life only through self-consciousness, do we not? I know I am alive because I speak, I think, I eat, I have various contradictory desires, conscious and unconscious, various compulsions, ambitions, and so on. It is only when I am conscious of these, that is, as long as I am self-conscious, that I know I am alive. And what do we mean by being self-conscious? Surely, I am self-conscious only when there is some kind of conflict; otherwise I am unconscious of myself. When I am thinking, making effort, arguing, discussing, putting it this way or that, I am self-conscious. The very nature of self-consciousness is contradiction. Consciousness is a total process; it is the hidden as well as the active, the open. Now, what does this process of consciousness mean, and where is it leading? We know birth and death, belief, struggle, pain, hope, ceaseless conflict. What is the significance of it all? One can find out its true significance only when the mind is capable of investigation, that is, when it is not anchored to any conclusion.

Q: Is it investigation, or re-investigation?

K: There is re-investigation only when the mind is tethered, repetitive, and therefore constantly re-investigating itself. To be free to investigate, to find out what is true, surely that requires a mind that is not held in the bondage of any conclusion. Now, can you and I find out what is the significance of this whole struggle with all its ramifications? If that is one's intention and one is serious, earnest, can one's mind have any conclusion about it? Must one not be open to this confusion? Must one not investigate it with a free mind to find out what is true? So what is important is not the problem but to see if it is possible for the mind to be free to investigate and find out the truth of it.

Can the mind be free from all conclusions? A conclusion is merely the response of a particular conditioning, is it not? Take the conclusion of reincarnation. Whether reincarnation is factual or not is irrelevant. Why do you have that conclusion? Is it because the mind is afraid of death? Such a mind, believing in a certain conclusion, which is the result of fear, hope, longing, is obviously incapable of discovering what is true with regard to death. So if we are at all serious, our first problem, even before we ask what this whole process of life means, is to find out whether the mind can be free from all conclusions.

Ojai, 6 August 1955

Questioner: All our troubles seem to arise from desire, but can we ever be free from desire? Is desire inherent in us, or is it a product of the mind?

Krishnamurti: What is desire? And why do we separate desire from the mind? Who is the entity that says, 'Desire creates problems; therefore I must be free from desire'? We have to understand what desire is, not ask how to get rid of desire because it creates trouble or whether it is a product of the mind. How does desire arise? I shall explain and you will see, but don't merely listen to my words. Actually experience the thing that we are talking about as we go along, and then it will have significance.

How does desire come into being? Surely it does that through perception or seeing, contact, sensation, and then desire. First you see a car, then there is contact, sensation, and finally the desire to own the car, to drive it. Please follow this slowly, patiently. Then, in trying to get that car, which is desire, there is conflict. So in the very fulfilment of desire there is conflict; there are pain, suffering, joy; and you want to hold the pleasure and discard the pain. This is what is actually taking place with each one of us. The entity created by desire, the entity who is identified with pleasure, says, 'I must get rid of that which is not pleasurable, which is painful'. We never say, 'I want to get rid of pain and pleasure'. We want to retain pleasure and discard pain, but desire creates both. Desire, which comes into being through perception, contact, and sensation, is identified as the 'me' who wants to hold on to the pleasurable and discard that which is painful. But the painful and the pleasurable are equally the outcome of desire, which is part of the mind; it is not outside the mind; and as long as there is an entity that says, 'I want to hold on to this and discard that', there must be conflict. Because we want to get rid of all the painful desires and hold on to those that are primarily pleasurable, worthwhile, we never consider the whole problem of desire. When we say, 'I must get rid of desire', who is the entity that is trying to get rid of something? Is not that entity also the outcome of desire?

Please, you must have infinite patience to understand these things. To fundamental questions there is no absolute answer of 'yes' or 'no'. What is important is to put a fundamental question not to find an answer; and if we are capable of looking at that fundamental question without seeking an answer, then that very observation of the fundamental brings about understanding.

So our problem is not how to be free from desires that are painful while holding on to those that are pleasurable but to understand the whole nature of desire. This brings up the question: what is conflict? And who is the entity that is always choosing between the pleasurable and the painful? The entity whom we call the 'me', the self, the ego, the mind that says, 'This is pleasure; that is pain. I will hold on to the pleasurable and reject the painful'—is not that entity still desire? But if we are capable of looking at the whole field of desire, and not in terms of keeping or getting rid of something, then we shall find that desire has quite a different significance.

Desire creates contradiction, and the mind that is at all alert does not like to live in contradiction; therefore it tries to get rid of desire. But if the mind can understand desire without trying to brush it away, without saying, 'This is a better desire, and that is a worse one. I am going to keep this and discard the other', if it can be aware of the whole field of desire without rejecting, choosing, condemning, then you will see that the mind is desire, is not separate from desire. If you really understand this, the mind becomes very quiet. Desires come, but they no longer have impact; they are no longer of great significance; they do not take root in the mind and create problems. The mind reacts—otherwise it is not alive—but the reaction is superficial and does not take root. That is why it is important to understand this whole process of desire in which most of us are caught. Being caught, we feel the contradiction, the infinite pain of it, so we struggle against desire, and the struggle creates duality. If we can look at desire without judgment, evaluation, or condemnation, then we shall find that it no longer takes root. The mind that gives soil to problems can never find that which is real. So the issue is not how to resolve desire but to understand it, and one can do that only when there is no condemnation of it.

New Delhi, 27 October 1963

BEFORE WE GO into the question of conflict and if it is at all possible to be free of it, we must, it seems to me, understand the structure of words, the meaning we give to a particular word, and discover through awareness of the word how the mind is caught in a web of them. Because we live, most of us, by formulas, by concepts, either self-created or handed down to us by society, which we call ideals, the necessity to have a certain pattern according to which we live. If you examine those formulas, ideas, concepts, and patterns, you will see that they are words, and those words control our activities, shape our thoughts, make us feel in a certain way. Words condition our thinking, our being.

A mind caught in words is incapable of being free. A mind functioning within the pattern of a formula is obviously a conditioned, slavish mind. It is incapable of thinking anew, afresh—and most of our thinking, most of our activity, our thought, is within the boundaries of words and formulas. Take a word like *God* or *love*. What extraordinary images, formulas, come to your mind! A man who would find if there is God, who would find out what love means, must obviously be free of all concepts, all formulas. And to be free of the formula, the concept, the mind refuses to break through, because there is fear. Fear takes shelter in words, and we battle over words. So the first thing for a man who would really go into this seriously, in order to discover if there is or is not a reality, something that is beyond the measure of words, is that he must absolutely understand words and be free of formulas.

❖

WHAT I WANT to discuss now is the conflict within and without and whether it is at all possible, living in this world, to be free of conflict totally, not partially. To be totally free of all conflict—is it at all possible? Don't say, 'It is' or 'It is not'. A serious mind does not take such a position; it inquires; and the mind must be free of conflict that creates confusion, contradiction, various forms of neurosis. If it is not free of this confusion, how can such a mind see, understand, observe? It can only spin a lot of words about truth, non-violence, God, bliss, Nirvana—and they have no meaning at all.

A mind that would find reality must be free of conflict at all levels of consciousness—which does not mean pursuing peace, retiring from the world, going to a monastery, or meditating under a tree; that is merely an escape. It must be free totally, at all the levels of consciousness, of all conflict so that the mind is clear. Only a mind that is clear can be free, and it is only in complete freedom that you can discover what is true.

So we have to investigate the anatomy, the structure of conflict. You are not listening to me, you are listening to your own consciousness. You are listening, observing, seeing the conflict in your own life—whether it is in the office, with your wife or husband, your children, your neighbour, your ideals—observing your own conflict. Because what we are concerned with is the revolution in you, not in me, revolution within each of us radically, at the very root of one's being. Otherwise change is superficial, an adjustment that has no value whatsoever. The world is undergoing tremendous changes not only technologically but morally, ethically; and merely to adapt oneself to a change does not bring about clarity of vision, clarity of mind. What brings about extraordinary clarity is when the mind has understood, totally, the whole

process of conflict within and without; and that very understanding brings freedom. Such a mind is clear, and in that clarity there
is beauty. Such a mind is the religious mind, not the phony mind
that goes to a temple, repeats words endlessly, performs cere-
monies ten thousand times—they have no meaning anymore.

What we are concerned with, then, is the understanding
of conflict—not how to get rid of conflict, not how to substitute
for conflict a series of formulas called peace or to resist or avoid
conflict but to understand it. I hope I am making myself clear
when I use the word *understand*. You know, to understand something is to live with it, and you cannot live with something if you
resist it, if you dissemble through your fear that which is a fact, if
you run away, or if, when you are in tremendous conflict within
yourself, you seek peace—which is just another form of escape. I
am using the word *understand* in a particular sense, that is, to face
the fact that you are in conflict and to live with it completely—not
to avoid it, not to escape. See if you can live with it, not translate
it, not bring in everyone's opinions about it, but live with it.

First of all, there is conflict not only at the conscious level
of the mind but also unconsciously, deep down. We are a mass of
conflicts, contradictions, not only at the level of thought but
also at the level that conscious thought has not penetrated.
This demands complete attention on your part. You are in conflict
whether you like it or not; your life is a misery, confusion, a series
of contradictions—violence and non-violence. All the saints have
destroyed you with their particular idiosyncrasies, particular patterns of violence and non-violence. To break all that, to find out
for yourself demands attention, an earnestness to go through right
to the very end of this question.

Everything we do brings conflict. We do not know a moment from schooldays till now when we are not in conflict. Going
to the office, which is a terrible bore, your prayers, your search for
God, your disciplines, your relationships—everything has in it a
seed of conflict. This is fairly obvious to any man who wants to
know himself; when he observes himself as in a mirror, he sees he

is in conflict. What does he do? Immediately he wants to run away from it or to find a formula that will absorb that conflict. What we are trying to do is to observe this conflict, not to run away from it.

Conflict arises when there is contradiction in our activity, our thought, our being, outwardly and inwardly. Conflict we accept as a way of progress. Conflict for us is a struggle. The adjustments, the suppressions, the innumerable contradictory desires, the various contradictory pulls, urges—all these create conflict within us. We are brought up to be ambitious, to make a success of life; and where there is ambition, there is conflict—this does not mean that you must go to sleep, that you must meditate. When you understand the very nature of conflict, a new energy comes, an energy that is uncontaminated by any effort, and that is what we are going to explore.

So first of all, to be aware that we are in conflict, not how to transcend it, not what to do about it, not how to suppress it, but to be aware and not do anything about it—that is necessary. We are going to do something about it later, but first not to do anything about what you have discovered, about the fact that you are in conflict, that you are trying to escape in different ways from that conflict. That is the fact; and when you remain with that fact for a few minutes, you will see how your mind resists remaining with it. It wants to run away, to act upon it, to do something about it. It can never live with that fact. To understand something, you have *got* to live with it; and to live with it, you have to be extremely sensitive. That is, to live with a beautiful tree or a picture or a person—to live with it is not to get used to it. The moment you get used to it, you have lost sensitivity to it. That is a fact. If I get used to the mountain where I live all my life, I am no longer sensitive to the beauty of line, the light, the shape, to the extraordinary brilliance of it in the morning or evening. I get used to it—which means I become insensitive to it. In the same way to live with an ugly thing demands equal sensitivity. If I get used to dirty roads, dirty thoughts, ugly situations, to putting up with things, I again become insensitive. To live with something, whether it is beautiful or ugly or a thing that brings sorrow—to live with it means to be sensitive to it and not get used to it. That is the first thing.

Conflict exists not only because we have contradictory desires, but all our education, all the psychological pressures of society bring about in us this division, this cleavage between what is and what should be, between the factual and the ideal. We are ridden with ideals. A mind that is clear has no ideals. It functions from fact to fact and not from idea to idea. We know conflict not only at the conscious level but also at the unconscious level. I do not want to discuss here what is conscious or what is unconscious; we will do that another day. We are concerned now with conflict, conflict throughout our total being, at both the conscious and the unconscious levels. There *is* conflict. Now, any effort to be free of it involves another conflict. That is fairly obvious, fairly logical. So the mind has to find a way of being free of conflict without effort. If I resist conflict or if I resist all the patterns, all the intimations that are involved in conflict, that very resistance is another contradiction and therefore a conflict.

Look, let me put it very simply. I realize I am in conflict. I am violent, and all the saints and all the books have said I must not be. So there are two contradictory things in me, violence and also that I must be non-violent. That is a contradiction, either self-imposed or imposed upon me by others. In that self-contradiction there is conflict. Now, if I resist, whether in order to understand or in order to avoid conflict, I am still in conflict. The very resistance creates conflict. That is fairly clear. To understand and be free of conflict, there must be no resistance to it, no escape from it. I must look at, listen to the whole content of conflict—with my wife, my children, with society, with all the ideas that I have. If you say it is not possible in this life to be free of conflict, then there is no further relationship between you and me. If you say it is possible, again there is no relationship between you and me. But if you say, 'I want to find out; I want to go into it; I want to tear down the structure of conflict that is being built in me and of which I am a part', then you and I have a relationship; then we can proceed together.

Every form of resistance, escape, and avoidance of conflict only increases it, and conflict implies confusion, brutality, hardness. A mind in conflict cannot be compassionate, have the clarity of compassion. So the mind has to be aware of conflict without resistance, avoidance, an opinion about it. In that very act a discipline is born—a flexible discipline, a discipline that is not based on any formula, any pattern, any suppression. That is to observe the whole content of conflict within, and that very observation brings with it naturally, effortlessly, a discipline. You must have this discipline. I am using the word *discipline* in the sense of clarity, in the sense of a mind that thinks precisely, healthily; and you cannot have such a mind if there is conflict.

Therefore the first essential is to understand conflict. Perhaps you will say, 'I am not free from conflict. Tell me how to be free from it'. That is the pattern you have learned. You want to be told how to be free from conflict, and you will pursue that pattern in order to be free from it and therefore still be in it. That is fairly simple. So there is no 'how'. Please understand this. There is no method in life. You have to live it. A man who has a method to achieve non-violence or some extraordinary state is merely caught in a pattern; and the pattern does produce a result, but it will not lead to reality. So when you ask, 'How am I to be free from conflict?' you are falling back into the old pattern—which indicates that you are still in conflict, that you have not understood; which means again that you have not lived clearly with the fact.

So being in conflict implies a confused mind, and you can see this all over the world. Every politician in the world is confused and has brought misery to the world. Equally, the saints have brought misery to the world. And if you are earnest and would be free of conflict, you have to abolish totally all authority in yourself, because for a man who wants to find truth there is no authority—neither the Gita, nor your saints, nor your leaders—nobody. That means you stand completely alone. To stand alone—that comes about when the mind is free from conflict.

You see, most of us want to avoid life, and we have found several ways and methods of avoiding it. Life is a total thing, not a partial thing. Life includes beauty, religion, politics, economics, relationships, quarrels, the misery, the torture, the agony of existence, the despair. All that is life, not just one part, one fragment of it, and you have to understand the totality of it. That requires a mind that is healthy, sane, clear. That is why you have to have a mind without conflict, a mind that has no mark of conflict, that has not been scratched. That is why conflict in any form can only be understood by being aware.

I mean by 'being aware' observing it. To observe demands that you should not look at it with an opinion. You should look at it but not with your ideas, your judgments, your comparison, your condemnation. If there is condemnation, resistance, you are not observing; therefore your concern then is not conflict. You cannot look at anything without an idea, and that becomes your problem. You want to observe conflict, but you cannot observe it if you bring in an opinion or idea or evaluation about that conflict or resist it. Your concern then is to find out why you resist—not how to understand conflict—why you resist. So you have moved away from conflict and become aware of your resistance. Why do you resist? You can find out why. For most of us, conflict has become a habit. It has made us so dull that we are not aware of it even. We have accepted it as a part of existence. When you do come upon it, see it as a fact, then you resist it or try to avoid it, to find a way out of it. To observe the fact that you resist is then far more important than to understand conflict—how you are avoiding it, bringing a formula to it. So you begin to observe your formulas, opinions, resistances. By being aware of all of them, you are breaking down your conditioning and are therefore able to face conflict.

So to understand conflict and therefore to be free of it, not eventually, not at the end of your life, not the day after tomorrow but immediately, totally—and it can be done—demands an astonishing faculty of observation, which is not to be cultivated because the moment you cultivate it you are back again in conflict. What is demanded is the immediate perception of the total process, the total content of consciousness—immediate observation and therefore seeing the truth of it. The moment you see the truth of it, you are out of it. You cannot see the truth of it, in any form whatsoever, at any level, if you try to resist, avoid, or impose upon it certain formulas that you have learned.

That brings up a very important question, which is: there is no time for change. Either you change now or never. I do not mean 'never' in the orthodox sense or in the Christian sense of 'eternally damned'. I mean: you change now in the active present—that active present may be tomorrow, but it is still the active present; and it is only in the active present that there is a mutation, not the day after tomorrow. This is very important to understand. We are so used to an idea, and then we try to put that idea into action. We first formulate logically or illogically—mostly illogically—an idea or an ideal and then try to put it into action. So there is a gap between action and the idea, a contradiction. The action is the living present, not the idea. The formula is merely a fixation; the active present is the action. So if you say, 'I must be free of conflict', that becomes an idea. There is a time interval between the idea and the action, and you hope that during that time interval some peculiar, mysterious action will take place that will bring about a change.

If you allow time, then there is no mutation. To understand is immediate, and you can only understand if you observe completely, with all your being—to listen to that aeroplane, to the hum of that with all your being, not to translate it, not say, 'That is an aeroplane' or 'How disturbing it is' or 'When I want to listen to him, that plane is going by'; then it becomes merely a distraction, a contradiction, and you are lost. To listen to that aeroplane with all your being is to listen to the speaker with all your being. There is no division between the two. There is a division only when you want to concentrate on what is being said, and that becomes a resistance. If you are completely *attentive*, then you are listening to that aeroplane and you are also listening to the speaker.

In the same way, if you are completely aware of the whole structure, the anatomy of conflict, then you will see that there is an immediate change. Then you are out of conflict completely. But if you say, 'Well, will it always be so, will I always be free of conflict?' then you are asking a foolish question. It indicates that you are not free of conflict, that you have not understood its nature. You only want to conquer it and be at peace.

A mind that has not understood conflict can never be at peace. It can escape to an idea, a word called peace, but that is not peace. To have peace demands clarity, and clarity can only come when there is no conflict of any kind—which is not a process of self-hypnosis. It is only the mind that has understood conflict with all its violence, all its insanity—and non-violence is a form of insanity because the mind has not understood violence—that can go very far. A mind that is forcing itself to be non-violent is violent. Most of your saints and teachers are full of violence; they do not know the clarity of compassion. And it is only the compassionate mind that can understand that which is beyond words.

Madras, 22 December 1965

Is it possible to end conflict in all our relationships—at home, in the office, in every area of our life? This does not mean that we retire in isolation, become a monk, or withdraw into some corner of our own imagination and fancy; it means living in this world to understand conflict. As long as there is conflict of any kind, our minds, hearts, brains cannot function to their highest capacity. They can do so only when there is no friction, when there is clarity. That is possible only when the totality of the mind—the physical organism, the brain cells, the whole thing called the mind—is in a state of non-conflict. Only then is it possible to have peace.

To understand that state, we must understand the everyday conflicts that mount up, the everyday battle within ourselves and with our neighbours, in the office, the family, between man and man, man and woman, and the psychological structure of this conflict, the 'me' of the conflict. Understanding, like seeing and listening, is one of the most difficult things. When you say, 'I understand something', you really mean not only that you have completely grasped the whole significance of what is being said but also that the very understanding is the action itself. You cannot understand if you are merely intellectually, verbally comprehending what is being said; if you merely listen intellectually—that is, verbally—surely that is not understanding. Or if you merely feel something emotionally, sentimentally, that also is not understanding.

You understand only when your total being comprehends—that is, when you do not look at anything fragmentarily, either only intellectually or emotionally, but totally.

So understanding the nature of conflict demands not the understanding of your particular conflict as an individual but understanding human conflict as a whole—which includes nationalism, class difference, ambition, greed, envy, the desire for position, prestige, the whole sense of power, domination, fear, guilt, anxiety, which involves death, meditation—the whole of life. To understand that, one must see, listen, not fragmentarily, but look at the vast map of life. One of our difficulties is that we function fragmentarily, we function partially—as an engineer, an artist, a scientist, a businessman, a lawyer, a physicist, and so on; and each fragment is in battle with the other fragment, despising it or feeling superior.

The question then is: how to look at the totality of life non-fragmentarily? When we look at the totality of life—not as a Hindu, a Moslem, a Catholic, a communist, a socialist, a professor, or a religious man—when we see the extraordinary movement of life, which includes everything, death, sorrow, misery, confusion, the utter lack of love and the image of pleasure that we have bred through centuries for ourselves, which dictates our values, our activities—when we see this vast thing, totally, then our response to that totality will be entirely different. It is this response, when we see totally the whole movement of life, that is going to bring about a revolution in ourselves, and this revolution is absolutely necessary. Human beings cannot go on as they have been, butchering each other, hating each other, dividing each other into countries, into all the petty, narrow, individualistic activities, because that way lie more misery, more confusion, and more sorrow.

So is it possible to see the totality of life, which is like a river moving endlessly, restlessly, with great beauty, moving because it has a great volume of water behind it? Can we see this life totally?

It is only when we see something totally that we understand it, and we cannot see it totally if there is self-centred activity that guides, shapes our action and our thoughts. It is the self-centred image that identifies with the family, the nation, ideological conclusions, with parties—whether political or religious. It is this centre that asserts it is seeking God, truth, and all the rest of it and that prevents comprehension of the whole of life. To understand this centre, actually what it is, needs a mind that is not cluttered up with concepts, conclusions. I must know *actually*, not theoretically, what I am. What I think, what I feel, my ambitions, greeds, envies, the desire for success, prominence, prestige, my greed, my sorrows—all that is what I am. I may think that I am God, I am something else; but that is still part of thought, part of the image that projects itself through thought. So unless you understand this thing not according to Sankara, Buddha, or anybody, unless you actually see what you are every day—the way you talk, the way you feel, the way you react, not only consciously but unconsciously—unless you lay the foundation there, how can you go very far? However far you may go, it will only be imagination, fantasy, deception, and you will be a hypocrite.

You have to lay this foundation—which is to understand what you are. That you can do only by watching yourself, not trying to correct it, not trying to shape it, not trying to say this is right or this is wrong, but by seeing what is actually taking place—which does not mean you become more self-centred. On the contrary, you become self-centred if you are merely correcting what you see, translating what you see according to your likes and dislikes; but if you merely observe, there is no intensification of the centre.

To see the totality of life needs great affection. You know, we have grown callous, and you can see why. In an overpopulated country—a country that is poor, both inwardly and outwardly, a country that has lived on ideas and not actuality, a country that has worshipped the past, with authority rooted in the past—naturally people are indifferent to what is actually going on. If you observe yourselves, you will see how little affection you have, affection being care. Affection means the sense of beauty, not external adornment only. The sense of beauty can come about only when there is great gentleness, great consideration, care that is the very essence of affection. When that is dry, our hearts are dry, and we fill them with words, ideas, quotations, with what has been said; and when we are aware of this confusion, we try to resurrect the past, we worship tradition, we go back. Because we do not know how to solve the present existence with all its confusion, we say, 'Let us go back; let us revert to the past; let us live according to some dead thing'. That is why, when confronted with the present, you escape into the past or some ideology or utopia, and, your heart being empty, you fill it with words, images, formulas, and slogans. Observe yourself, and you will know all this.

So to bring about naturally, freely, this total mutation in the mind itself demands great, serious attention. We do not want to attend, because we are afraid of what may happen if we really think about the actual, daily facts of our life. We are really afraid to examine; we would rather live blindly, suffocated, miserable, unhappy, trivial, and therefore empty and meaningless lives; and, life being meaningless, we try to invent significance in life. Life has no significance. Life is meant to be lived, and in that very living one begins to discover the reality, the truth, the beauty of life. To discover the truth, the beauty of life, you must understand the total movement of it, and to do that you have to end all this fragmentary thinking and way of life. You have to cease to be a Hindu, not only in name but inwardly; you have to cease to be a Moslem or a Buddhist or a Catholic with all the dogmas, because these things are dividing people, dividing your own minds, your own hearts.

Strangely, you will listen to all this, you will listen for an hour, and you will go home and repeat the pattern. You will repeat the pattern endlessly, and this pattern is based essentially on pleasure.

So you have to examine your own life voluntarily, not because the government influences you or somebody tells you to.

You have voluntarily to examine it, not condemn it, not say this is right or this is wrong but look. When you do look in that way, you will find that you look with eyes that are full of affection—not with condemnation, not with judgment, but with care. You look at yourself with care and therefore with immense affection—and it is only when there is great affection and love that you see the total existence of life.

Rome, 31 March 1966

Is it possible to find a way of daily living that is basically and radically free and therefore revolutionary? There is only one revolution for me, and that is religious revolution. The others—economic, social, political—are not revolutions. The only revolution is the religious mind in revolt, not as a reaction, but a mind that has established a way of life in which there is no contradiction. All our lives are in contradiction and therefore in conflict, either conflict born of trying to conform, conflict through seeking fulfilment, or conflict engendered by social influence. Human beings have lived in this state of conflict for the whole of known history.

Everything they touch they turn into conflict, within and without. Either it's a war between people, or life as a human being is a battlefield within. We all know this constant, everlasting struggle, outwardly and inwardly. Conflict does produce a certain result by the use of the will, but it is never creative. To live, to flower in goodness, there must be peace, not economic peace, the peace between two wars, the peace of politicians negotiating treaties, the peace that the church talks about or the organized religious preach of, but the peace that one has discovered for oneself. It is only in peace that we can flower, grow, be, and function. It cannot come into being when there is conflict of any kind, whether conscious or unconscious.

Is it possible to live a life without conflict in the modern world, with all the strain, struggle, pressures, and influences in the social structure? That is really living, the essence of a mind that is inquiring seriously. The question whether there is God, whether there is truth, whether there is beauty can come only when this is established, when the mind is no longer in conflict.

Questioner: How is one to avoid this conflict?

Krishnamurti: You can't avoid conflict. You have to understand its nature. Conflict is one of the most difficult things to understand. We have tried to avoid conflict, so we take to drink, sex, church, organized religion, social activities, superficial amusement—every form of escape. We have tried to avoid conflict, but we haven't been able to. The very avoidance is contributory to conflict.

Q: Could you say something about the nature of conflict?

K: We'll go into that. First let us see the fundamental, radical necessity of freedom and peace. We don't know what it means yet. We can see, perhaps intellectually, the necessity of a mind, a heart, the whole structure of a human being not having conflict, because then there is peace. That peace is really a form of moral behaviour, because a mind that is not peaceful cannot behave, cannot have right relationship; and right relationship is conduct, virtue, morals, all the rest of it.

If both of us understand the necessity of ending conflict—understand it even verbally, for the moment—then we can proceed; then we can begin to investigate what conflict is, why it comes into being, and whether it is at all possible to end it by insisting upon a factor called the will. Let's begin slowly. It's a tremendous subject; we can't brush it off in an afternoon. What is conflict, both outwardly and inwardly? We can see that outwardly wars are the result of nationalities, economic pressures, religious and personal prejudices. There have been religious wars throughout the history of the world. Perhaps Buddhism has not contributed to war, though recently Buddhist priests have burned themselves, but it is totally against the teaching. They are told never to touch politics, but politics is the new oracle; it provides the intoxication of nationalism. We can see then the outward contributory factors of war, ideologies; we don't have to go into that.

Then there is inward conflict, which is much more complex. Why is there conflict in us? We are examining; we are not saying that we should or should not be without conflict. We are examining it; and to do that we must be very clear in our thinking, intensely acute and aware in observing the whole nature and significance of conflict. Why is there conflict? What do we mean by that word *struggle?* We are examining the meaning of the word, not what brings about conflict. When are we at all conscious of this word, of the fact? Only when there is pain, a contradiction, the pursuit of pleasure and its denial. I am aware of conflict when my form of pleasure in fulfilment, in ambition of various forms, is thwarted. When the pleasure of ambition is frustrated, then I am conscious of conflict, but as long as that pleasure continues unhindered, I have no sense of conflict at all. There is pleasure in conformity. I want to conform to society because it pays me; it gives me profit. For security, for a means of livelihood, to become famous, to be recognized, to be somebody in society, I must conform to the norm, to the pattern set by society. As long as I am conforming to it completely, which is a great pleasure, there is no conflict; but there is conflict the moment there is a distraction from that conformity.

Rajghat, 10 December 1967

Questioner: Sir, you have told us about care, affection, and love, but how is it possible for two nations to care about each other?

Krishnamurti: Obviously they cannot. When you are going north and I am going south, how can there be care or attention or love? When, as one nation, you want one piece of property and another nation wants the same property, how can there be care or love? There can only be war, which is what is happening. As long as there are nationalities, sovereign governments controlled by the army and the politicians, with their idiotic ideologies, their separateness, there must be war. As long as you worship a particular rag called a flag, and I worship another rag of another colour, obviously we are going to fight each other.

Only when there are no nationalities, no divisions such as Christians, Buddhists, Hindus, Moslems, communists, or capitalists will there be no war. Only when man gives up his petty beliefs and prejudices, his worship of his own particular family, and all the rest of it is there a possibility of peace in the world. That peace can come about only when the whole world is organized, and it cannot be organized economically or socially as long as there is division. That means that there must be a universal language and planning—which none of you want. But as long as you keep your particular beliefs, nationalities, gods, and gurus, you are bound to be at war with one another. It is like a man pretending to be brotherly when all the time he hates people.

Brockwood Park, 8 September 1970

Krishnamurti: Before we try to find out how to educate children so that they do not conform, or do conform, shouldn't we find out whether we ourselves, the educators, the parents, the teachers are, as human beings, conforming? Are we imitating, following a certain pattern, accepting formulas, and fitting life to that formula? All that implies, surely, conformity, accepting authority, having a formula, principle, or belief according to which one lives, or rejecting the outer patterns of conformity imposed on us through culture, education, the impact of social influences. We may also have our own patterns of inward conformity and accept and conform to them—conforming both outwardly and inwardly.

Am I aware that I am conforming? Not that one should, or should not, but first let's begin to find out if one is conforming. What does it mean? All the structure of language is a form of acceptance of a pattern of speech, of thought, conditioned by words and so on. One can see one conforms there. Also, one does conform to outward social patterns: short hair, long hair, beard, no beard, trousers, miniskirts, long skirts, all the rest of that. And inwardly is one conforming, following an image one has built about oneself, a conclusion, a belief, a pattern of conduct? Is one aware of all this? Not that one should or should not imitate, but is one aware that there is this outward and inward conformity all the

time? Because if one is conforming, there is obviously no freedom, and without freedom there is no intelligence.

So to inquire within, look at oneself quite objectively
without any sentimentality, without saying this is right or this is
wrong, just to observe and find out at what depth one is conforming. At a very superficial level, or does one conform right through
one's being? It is really quite a complex subject, this—because we
have been educated to divide life as the 'me' and the 'not me', as
the observer and the thing observed being something separate.
Basically that is one of the patterns of conformity; that's the way
we have been brought up. When I say, 'I am a Hindu', it is conforming to the pattern of the particular culture and society in
which this particular mind has been cultured, brought up. Is one
doing that? This is really quite extraordinarily interesting if one
goes into it very deeply.

First let us see how you and I conform. If we as the educators, parents don't understand what it means to conform, how
can we help another to be free of conformity or say you must conform? We must be clear in ourselves. Let's not put the cart before
the horse!

You see, this is really very subtle and has great depth
if you go into it. Memory, the cultivation of memory, is what
education is at present, what the facts are, and this and that
technology. The path of knowledge, you follow, is to conform. Following the past, accepting a tradition, calling oneself a German, a
Russian, an Englishman, is conforming, and the revolt against that
becomes another pattern of conformity. Therefore all reaction is a
form of conformity. I don't know if you accept all this. I don't like
the particular system, the capitalist or the communist system. I revolt against it because I want a different kind of system; and that
different kind of system is the outcome of these two particular systems, and I prefer that and therefore I am conforming to that.

So in inquiring into this question—not how to bring up
children; we will come to that later—one has to find out in oneself
these patterns of conformity, imitation.

Questioner: Sir, if we do not follow these systems that exist in our society, how can we educate our children to pass examinations?

K: Let's not talk about the children for the moment. Let us talk about ourselves, who are responsible for these unfortunate children, whether *we* are conforming. If we are, then whatever our relationship with the children, we will always subtly or brutally bring about an educational system that will make the child or the grown-up or the adolescent conform. This is so simple. If I am blind, I can't lead, I can't look, I can't help another. We are more or less blind if we don't know at what depths we are conforming.

Q: But isn't knowledge of these depths a continuous process? Doesn't it become more precise?

K: It does, sir, it does become very precise. If we could please give a little attention to this. Are you conforming? Obviously, when I put on trousers, I am conforming. When I go to India and I put on different clothes, I am conforming. When I have my hair cut short, I am conforming. When I have my hair long, or an enormous beard, I am conforming.

Q: But is it not much more a matter of looking at oneself and the outer world as two separate things?

K: I said that. The division as the 'me' and the 'not me', the outer and the inner, this division is another form of conformity. Let's get at the principle of it, not at the peripheral conformities, but at the root. Why does the human mind conform? Does that human mind know it is conforming? In asking that question, we will find out, rather than inquiring about the peripheral conformity, the borders of conformity. That's a sheer waste of time. Once the central issue is understood, then we can deal with the outer, the peripheral conformity.

Q: Sir, I feel very insecure if I don't follow a certain pattern.

K: He says, if I don't follow a certain pattern, established by a particular society and culture, whether communist, Finnish, German, this or that, Catholic, I shall be thrown out. Right? Imagine what happens in Russia, under the Soviet tyranny, though they call it a people's democracy, all that bilge, I shall be wiped out, I shall be sent to a mental hospital and given drugs to become normal. So before we say, what shall I do in a particular culture where conformity is the pattern, before we even put that question we should find out for ourselves whether we are conforming and what it means. You see, you are always discussing what to do in a given structure of society. That's not the question. The question is, is one aware, does one know that one is conforming? Is that conformity peripheral, superficial, or is it very profound? Until you answer this question, you won't be able to deal with the question whether to fit into a particular society that demands conformity.

Q: I act in a certain way. How do I know if I am conforming or not?

K: We will have to find that out, sir. Let's go into it. Let's take time and patience in finding out. Don't let us ask peripheral questions like what to do.

Q: It seems possible that like any other species we have a natural and instinctive desire to conform.

K: Yes. Why? We know this. This whole process of education, all our upbringing is to conform. Why? Do look at it. The animal conforms.

Q: To preserve the species.

Questioner 2: To keep together.

Questioner 3: To preserve the group.

K: To preserve the group, to have security, to be safe. That's why we conform. Does that conformity lead to security? We say it does, but does it? I mean, to call oneself an American, an Indian, a Japanese, or an Indonesian does seem to give a sense of security. To identify oneself with a particular community appears to give security. But does it? When you call yourself a German and I call myself a Jew or an Englishman, this very division is one of the major causes of war, which means no security. Where there is division that comes about through identification with a particular community, hoping that community will give security, it is the very beginning of the destruction of security. This is so clear.

Q: Then you feel that the idea of any community is one that would detract from . . .

K: No, sir, no sir. We are saying the desire to conform, the urge, the instinct to conform, comes about through the hope of security, wanting to be secure, safe, certain physically. Is that a fact? History—not that I am a historian—has shown that when you call yourself a Catholic and I call myself a Protestant, we have murdered each other in the name of God and all the rest of it. So the mind seeking security through conformity destroys that very security. That's clear, isn't it? So when that's clear, we have finished with identification with a community through which we hope to be secure. That thinking, looking at it that way, is finished. Once you see the poisonous nature of this division between communities and of your identifying with a community in the hope of security, when you see that very clearly, the truth of it, you no longer want security through a community, through nationality, through identification with a particular group.

Q: Is there not another point, the feeling of belonging?

K: Yes, sir. I belong to a particular group. It gives me satisfaction;

it makes me feel warm inside; it makes me feel safe. That is the same thing.

Q: It is much more than being safe. It's a nice feeling.

K: Yes, sir, which is what? A nice feeling—I belong to this community at Brockwood. It gives me a nice feeling. What does that mean? It means I want to belong to something. Why? Sir, let us tear this apart and look at it. Why do I want to feel comfortable with a blasted little community? Sorry!

Q: I feel insufficient in myself.

K: What does that mean? In myself I am insufficient; I am lonely; I am a poor, unhappy, haggard, miserable entity; and I say, my God, if I could identify myself with a large community, I would lose myself in that. This is so simple.

Q: We want communion.

K: With whom?

Q: With other people.

K: How do you have communion with other people when you are seeking security through other people?

Q: It is not a matter of security.

K: Sir, look. I feel comfortable, happy, with a small group of people, a particular community. Why? You have to answer this question. Why do I feel comfortable with a particular group of people?

Q: Because I am frightened by the others.

K: I am not only frightened by the others.

Q: No.

K: No, then what? I don't like the others. I don't like their looks, their smell, their clothes, their beards, their hair. I like this group. That group gives me a great sense of warmth.

Q: We want expansion.

K: Expanding what? What am I expanding? My loneliness, my fear, my misery, my lack of certainty? When I am clear, certain, you know, vital, I don't want to identify myself with anything. I don't know why we waste time on this thing. We ought to go much deeper than this. Which is, any form of identification with a group, however comfortable, however satisfying, implies not only psychological well-being, psychological well-being in division, and therefore destruction, but also brings about a conformity of the group as against another group. So our question is: why do we conform, and do I know I am conforming? Please, do stick to those two things. Do you know you are conforming? When you call yourself an Englishman or a Frenchman, aren't you conforming? When you call yourself a Catholic, Protestant, communist, the Panthers, and all the rest, aren't you conforming? And when you are aware that you are conforming, peripherally or superficially, the next question is, why? If you say it is to be safe, secure, then you see the dangers of that security. There is no security when you identify yourself with a group, however satisfying it is. So isn't that clear? We can push it aside, finish with it. Any form of identification with a group, however satisfactory, however comforting, does not bring security. So I will never look for security in a group. Can't we finish with that?

Q: Yes.

K: Wait. Yes, but *do it!*

Q: It doesn't always seem that we are identifying when we are doing it, but that we are working together and then it slips over somehow.

K: Yes. The question is, we may think we are working together, not necessarily identifying together. Is co-operation imitation, conformity? Please go into it a little bit. Am I co-operating with you about something? About a principle, about utopia, about a series of ideations, or co-operating with you because you bring enlightenment, or have I the spirit of co-operation in which there is no conformity? If I am co-operating about something because I hope through that co-operation I will gain a personal profit, then it's not co-operation. But if I have the spirit of co-operation, the feeling . . .

Q: I go beyond the me.

K: Madam, that's just it. Do I have the spirit of co-operation, the feeling? So let's come back. I must come back to this thing, which is, does one know that one is conforming, why one is conforming, and what is the necessity to conform?

Q: It presents an image of sameness.

K: No, look at it, sir. Are you conforming? I am sorry to push it. Are you conforming? When you take drugs—not you, I am talking generally, it's not my concern whether you take them or not, sir—isn't that conformity? When you drink, smoke, isn't that conformity?

Q: It seems that you can't talk about an action, saying it is a conforming action. You have to talk about the mind.

K: Sir, we did just now. Why does the mind conform?

Q: You can say the mind conforms, but can you say that if such and such an action is conforming, that it is done by a conforming mind?

K: Do you know that you are conforming through the action of conformity? I am doing something, and the doing of it reveals that I am conforming. Or without action I know one is conforming. You see the difference? Do I know that I am hungry because you tell me? Or do I know for myself I am hungry? Do I know I am conforming because I see the action of conformity going on? I wonder if I am making myself clear? Do please go with me.

Do I know through action that I am conforming, or do I know I am conforming but not through action? There are two different kinds of knowledge. The discovery that I am conforming through action leads to the correction of action. Right? I discover I am conforming through a particular act, and then I say to myself, to change, to bring about a change in conformity, I must act differently. So I lay emphasis on action, not on the movement that brings about action. This is clear. So I want to be clear, before I talk about action, of the nature of conformity.

Q: Sir, I don't understand how you can observe the nature of conformity without the action to reveal it.

K: That's just it. I cannot find out the nature of conformity without being aware of the action that is the result of conformity. Right?

Q: Conformity is connected with an objective.

K: Sir, how do you know that you are conforming?

Q: Through observation.

K: Through observation. Do be clear. Wait a minute. Through observation, you say. The observer watching action says, 'I am conforming'. Right? Is not the very observer the result of centuries of conformity?

Q: Yes.

K: Therefore he is watching, not action, but watching himself conforming.

Q: Yes.

K: He is the source of all conformity, not what he is doing. What he is doing is the result of the flow of conformity, as the observer, the censor, the Englishman, the traditionalist, and so on. So when we are asking the questions who is conforming, what is conformity, and why does one conform, I think the answer to all that lies in the observer. The observer is the censor. Now the censor becomes aware of himself condemning or justifying. That condemnation or justification is the result of his conformity to the pattern of a particular culture in which he has been brought up. There is the whole thing.

Brockwood Park, 31 August 1974

WE HAVE TO observe, obviously, not only our lives but also what is going on around us—the conflict, violence, the extraordinary sense of despair, sorrow, meaningless existence. To escape from that we resort to all kinds of fanciful, sectarian beliefs. Gurus are multiplying like mushrooms in autumn all over the world. They are bringing their own particular fancy, their traditions, and imposing them on others. That is not religion; that is sheer nonsense, traditional acceptance of what has been, of what is dead. So it becomes very important not only that we bring about a change in the world outside us but also a total psychological revolution inwardly. That seems to me the most urgent and necessary thing. That will bring about, naturally and inevitably, a change in the social structure, in our relationships, our whole activity.

So the first thing, it seems to me, is the act of observation—to observe, to observe without the observer. We will go into this because it is quite difficult.

To observe, not as an Englishman, an American, a Hindu, Buddhist, Catholic, Protestant, communist, socialist, or what you will, but to observe without these conditioning attitudes, to observe without traditional acceptance, to observe without the 'me' interfering with the observation. The 'me' that is the result of the past, all our traditions, our education, of our social, environmental, economic influence—this 'me' that interferes with observation.

Now is it possible to totally eliminate in observation this activity of the 'me'? Because it is the 'me' that separates and thereby brings about conflict in our relationships with each other.

Is it possible to observe this whole phenomenon of existence without the traditional 'me', with its prejudices, opinions, judgments, its desires, pleasures, and fears? If it is not, we are caught in the same old trap of slight reformation in the same area, with a little more experience, a little more expansive knowledge, and so on, but always remaining in the same area unless there is a radical understanding of the whole structure of the 'me'. It seems to me that this is so obvious, yet most of us are apt to forget it; most of us are so burdened with our own opinions, judgments, and individualistic attitudes that we are incapable of perceiving the whole. In the perception of the whole lies our salvation. I mean by the word *salvation* a different way of living, acting, thinking so that we can live totally at peace within ourselves without conflict, without problems.

That is what we are going to talk over together: whether the human mind, so conditioned, through time, evolution, all the experiences, a great deal of knowledge, whether such a mind, your mind, our mind, our consciousness can go beyond itself. Not in theory, not in fancy, not in romantic experiences but *actually*, without any sense of illusion. Because our consciousness is the consciousness of the world. I think this is important to understand. Our consciousness with its content is the consciousness of every human being in the world. We may vary a little bit here and there, different colour, different shape, different form, but the content of our consciousness is essentially the consciousness of the world. If that content can be changed, then the consciousness of the world can be changed. Are we meeting each other over this; are we talking the same language?

If I can change the content of my consciousness, it will obviously affect the consciousness of others. And this content makes up my consciousness. The content is not separate from consciousness. As a human being I live in this world with all the

travail, misery, confusion, suffering, violence, the separate nationalities, with their conflicts, wars, brutalities, with all the calamities
that are going on. That is part of my and part of your consciousness—the consciousness trained to accept saviours, teachers,
gurus, authority. Now can all that consciousness be transformed?
If it can be transformed, what is the way to do it? Obviously not a
method. Method implies a preconceived plan or system invented
by somebody whom you respect or think has got the final answer,
and according to that method you conform. Which we have done,
and therefore it is still within the same pattern. So if one rejects
conformity to any pattern, method, end, doing so not through resistance but through understanding, having an insight into the
foolishness of conformity, then the mind comes across a much
more difficult problem—fear. Please, this is not mere talk, but
rather we are sharing, and I keep on repeating it, sharing this
thing. Sharing implies attention. Sharing implies the necessity,
the urgency of understanding, not intellectually, not verbally, but
understanding with our minds, our hearts, our whole being.

As we said, our consciousness with its content is the consciousness of the world, because wherever you go people are suffering. There is poverty, misery, brutality; this is part of our daily
life. There is social injustice, the tremendously wealthy and the
poor. Wherever one goes this is an absolute fact. Each one of us is
suffering, is caught in all kinds of problems, sexual, personal, collective, and so on. This conflict goes on throughout the world in
every human being. Our consciousness is theirs. Therein lies compassion, not intellectual compassion but actual passion for this
whole human being, who is caught in this extraordinary travail.

When one looks at consciousness without interpreting it
as good or bad, noble or ignoble, beautiful or ugly, just observes it
without any interpretation, then you will see for yourself that there
is a tremendous sense of fear, insecurity, lack of certainty, and because of that insecurity we escape into every form of neurotic security. Please do observe it in yourselves, not merely accept what the
speaker is saying. Also, when you observe it, who is the observer?

Who is the observer that is observing this whole phenomenon? Is the observer different from the thing observed? Is the thinker different from the thought? Is the experiencer different from the thing he experiences? It seems to me that is one of the basic things that we have to understand. To us there is a division between the observer and the observed, and this division brings about conflict. Wherever there is division, there must be conflict.

So one must be very clear, it seems to me, about these questions: who is the observer, and is the observer different from the thing observed? I look at my consciousness—I don't know if you have ever tried to look at your consciousness. Look at it as though you were looking at yourself in the mirror. To look at all the conscious as well as unconscious activities of your consciousness, which is within the field of time, within the area of thought. Now, can one observe it? Or does one observe it as though it were something outside oneself? If you do observe it, is the observer who is observing different from the thing observed? And what makes him different? Are we meeting each other? We are taking a journey together. Don't let me walk by myself, please; we are all together in this.

What is the observer? What are the structure and nature of the observer? Is the observer the past, with his experiences, his knowledge, his accumulated hurts, his sorrows, and so on? Is the observer the past? Is the observer the 'me'? Is the observer, being the past, capable of looking at what is going on around him now? That is, if I am living in the past, with the remembrances, the hurts, the sorrows, all the knowledge the mind has accumulated— and all knowledge always is in the past—I observe with that mind. And when I observe with that mind, I am always looking through eyes that have been wounded, that have remembered the things of the past. I am always looking through the past, through accumulated tradition, and so I am never looking at the present. There is a division between the observer who is the past and the active, moving, living present. So there is a conflict between the observer and the observed.

Can the mind observe without the observer? This is not a conundrum, a trick, not something to speculate about. You can see it for yourself; you can have an insight into the reality: that is, the observer can never observe. He can observe what he wants to observe; he observes according to his desires, his fears, his inclinations, romantic demands, and so on. The observed becomes totally different when the observer is himself totally different. If I have been brought up as a Catholic, a Buddhist, a Hindu, or God knows what else, and I observe life, this extraordinary movement of life with my conditioned mind, my beliefs, my fears, my saviours, I am observing not 'what is'; I am observing my own conditioning and therefore never observe 'what is'.

When I observe, is the observer different from me? Or the observer *is* the observed—you understand? Which eliminates conflict altogether. Because you see our lives, our education, our way of living are based on conflict—all our relationships, our activities, the way we live, the way we think spring from this everlasting conflict between you and me, between each other, outwardly as well as inwardly. And the religious life so far has heightened conflict, made it a life of torture—you must come to God, or whatever, through conformity, acceptance of a belief—which are all forms of conflict. And a mind that is in conflict is obviously not a religious mind.

So one comes to the point: can the mind, your mind, observe without the observer? That becomes extremely arduous because it raises the whole question of fear. There are not only the conscious fears but the deep-rooted fears. Now, can the mind be free of fear? Not a few fears or the fears one is conscious of but the entire structure of fear, conscious as well as unconscious? Perhaps you would say that it is not possible, no human being can live in this world without fear. Now, we are asking whether a mind that lives in fear—fear of tomorrow, of what has been, of what might be, of what is, fear in relationship, of loneliness, a dozen forms of fear, the most absurd fears, and the most tragic fears—can the mind be free of all that?

Now how do you investigate fear? I am afraid of a dozen things. How do I investigate and be free of fear, bearing in mind that the observer is the observed—fear is not different from the observer. The observer is part of the fear, obviously. So how is the mind to be free of fear? Because with the burden of fear one lives in darkness, and from fear arise aggression, violence, all the neurotic activities that go on not only in the religious field but in daily relationship. So for a healthy, sane mind that is whole there must be freedom from fear. Not partial freedom but total freedom: there is no such thing as partial freedom. So the observer is fear himself, and when he observes fear as something separate from himself, there is conflict. Then he tries to overcome, suppress it, escape from it, and so on. But when one has the insight, this truth that the observer is the observed, then what takes place?

Let me put it differently: I am angry—is that anger different from me? Me, the observer, who says, 'I am angry?' Or that anger is part of me? It seems so simple. And when I realize that the observer is the observed, that the anger that I recognize is part of me, not something apart, then what am I to do with that anger? I am not separate from that anger. I *am* anger. I am not separate from violence. I *am* that violence. That violence has come about through my fear; that fear has brought about aggression. So I am all that. Then what takes place?

Let us look at it a little more: when I am angry each response, which I call anger, is recognized, because I have been angry before. So the next time I am angry I recognize it, and that makes the anger still stronger because I am looking at this new response with the recognition of a previous anger. So I am merely recognizing anger. I am not going beyond it; I am merely recognizing it each time. So can I, can the mind, observe that anger without recognition, without using the word *anger*, which is a form of recognition? We are violent human beings in so many ways; we may have a gentle face and quiet voice, but deeply we are violent people. There are violent activities, violent speech, and all the rest of it. Now is that violence different from me, from the observer? I see that the observer is part of that violence. It is not that the observer is non-violent, therefore he looks at violence, but the observer himself is part of that.

Then what will he do? I am part of that violence, and before I have separated myself from that violence, saying, 'I must suppress it; I must conquer it; I must go beyond it', and therefore there is a conflict between that and myself. Now I have eliminated that absurdity, I see the fact that I am violent, that the very structure of me is violent. Then what takes place? Obviously, there is no desire to overcome it because I am part of that. There is no question of my trying to overcome, to suppress it; suppression, overcoming, escaping are a wastage of energy—aren't they? Now when the observer is the observed, I have all that energy that was dissipated before by escaping, by suppression. Now I have that tremendous energy that comes about when the observer is the observed, and that energy can go beyond violence.

We need energy, don't we, to do anything. I need energy to go beyond violence, and I have wasted that energy through suppression, conformity, rationalization, through all kinds of escapes and justifications. When I see the observer is the observed and all that energy is concentrated, when that total energy is there, there is no violence. It is only fragments that create violence.

Questioner: There is interaction.

Krishnamurti: Not interaction, sir. Let's stick to one thing. Don't bring in interaction yet; we will come to that. Sir, look, human beings throughout the world have tried, in the old traditional way, to overcome violence, anger, through rationalization, justification, escapes, all kinds of neurotic activities, and we have not gone beyond violence, we have not gone beyond anger, brutality, and all the rest of it. Now can the mind go beyond it? Once and for all finish with violence? It is possible only when we realize the observer is the observed, because in observation there is then no escape, no interpretation, no rationalization, just the thing is, and therefore you have the energy to go beyond it. Do this, and you will see it. But you must first understand the reason, the logic, the truth that the observer is the observed.

When you look at another—wife, husband, girlfriend, boyfriend, and so on—are you different from what you observe, from the person you observe? The form, a man or a woman, may be different, the sex may be different, but psychologically is your consciousness different from hers or his? Do investigate this as we go along. When you observe, you are observing your own image, not observing another. The image that you have built through various interactions, the image you have built about her or him, that image is looking. This is so obvious, isn't it? So when one really understands, not verbally, not intellectually, but as an actuality, as something true, that the observer is the observed, all conflict comes to an end, and our relationship with each other therefore undergoes a radical transformation.

So can the mind observe fear? Let us go back to that: your fear of death, of life, of loneliness, of darkness, of being nobody, of not becoming a great howling success, of not being a leader, a writer, this or that, ten different things. First of all, is one aware of it? Or one leads such a superficial life, everlastingly talking about something else, that one is never aware of oneself, of one's own fears. Then, if one becomes aware of those fears, at what level do you become aware? Is it an intellectual awareness of your fears, or are you actually aware of your fears—aware in the sense that you are aware of the colour of the jersey next to you? Are you aware of your fear at the deeper levels, the hidden recesses, of your mind, and if they are hidden, how are they to be exposed? Must you go to an analyst? And the analyst is yourself. He needs to be analysed, too; otherwise, he wouldn't be an analyst!

So how do you uncover this whole structure, the intricacies of fear? You know this is a tremendous problem, not just to be listened to for two or three minutes and then forgotten—to find out for oneself whether it is possible to expose all the fears or there is only one central fear, which has many branches. And when one sees the central fear, the branches begin to wither away. Now, how do you approach this? From the periphery or from the centre? If the mind can understand the root of fear, then the branches, the various aspects of fear, have no meaning; they wither away. So what is the root of fear? Can you look at your fear? Look at it now, invite it—naturally you are not afraid here, but you know what your fears are: loneliness, not being loved, not being beautiful, losing your position, your job, your this or that, ten different things. Now by looking at one fear, at your particular fear, you can then see the root of that fear, and not only the root of that fear but the root of all fear. By observing one fear, in the sense that the observer is the observed, you will see for yourself that through one fear you discover the root of all fear. Suppose one is afraid—of what?

Q: Loneliness.

K: Loneliness. One is afraid of loneliness. Now, first of all, have you looked at loneliness, or is that an idea of which you are frightened? Not the fact of loneliness but the idea of loneliness—you see the difference? Which is it? The idea frightens you, or the actuality frightens you?

Q: Not separate, is it?

K: No sir, look. I have an idea of loneliness. The idea being the rationalization of thought that says, 'I don't know what it is, but I am afraid of it'. Or I know what loneliness is not as an idea but as an actuality. I know it when I am in a crowd and suddenly feel that I am not related to anything, that I am absolutely disassociated, lost, cannot rely on anybody. All my moorings have been cut away, and I feel tremendously lonely, frightened. That is an actuality. But the idea *about* it is not an actuality, and most of us, I am afraid, have an idea about it.

So if it is not an idea but an actuality, what is loneliness? Aren't we breeding it all the time—by our self-centred activity, by this tremendous concern with ourselves, our looks, attitudes, opinions, judgments, position, status, our importance, all that? All that is a form of isolation. We have done this, throughout the day, for years, and suddenly we find ourselves utterly isolated; our beliefs and God and everything go away. There is this sense of tremendous isolation, which cannot be penetrated; and that naturally brings great fear. Now I observe, in my life, in my daily life, that my activities, my thoughts, my desires, my pleasures, my experiences are more and more isolating. And the ultimate sense is death—that is a different point. So I observe it. I observe it in my daily movements, daily activities. And in the observation of this loneliness, the observer is part of, is essentially that loneliness. So the observer is the observed. And therefore he cannot possibly escape from it. He cannot cover it up, try to fill it with good works or whatever, going off to church and meditation and all the rest of it. So the observer is the observed. What happens then? You have eliminated conflict altogether, haven't you? Not trying to escape from it, not trying to cover it up, not trying to rationalize it, you are faced with it, you *are* that. When you are confronted with it completely and there is no escape and you are that, then there is no problem, is there? There is no problem because then there is no sense of loneliness at all.

So can you observe your fear? Through one fear trace the very root of all fear? That is, through this sense of loneliness, haven't you traced the root of fear? I am lonely. I know what that means not as an idea but as an actuality. I know what hunger is as an actuality, not because somebody has told me what hunger is. There is this extraordinary sense of loneliness, isolation. Isolation is a form of resistance, a form of exclusion. I am fully aware of that, and I am also aware that the observer is the observed. And there is fear there, deep-rooted fear; and through one factor of fear, of loneliness, I have been able to find out, look at, the central fact of fear, which is the existence of the observer. If the observer is not, the observer being the past, his opinions, judgments, evaluations, rationalizations, interpretations, all the tradition, if that is not, where is fear?

If the 'me' is not, where is the fear? But we are educated religiously, and in colleges, schools, and universities, to assert, to cultivate the 'me' as the observer. I am a Catholic, a Protestant, British, I am this, I am that, all the rest of it. And by looking at one fear, the mind has been able to look and trace the central fact of fear, which is the existence of the observer, the 'me'. And can I live in this world without that 'me'? When everything around me is an assertion of the 'me', the culture, the works of art, business, politics, religion, everything around me says *cultivate the 'me'*. In such a culture, such a civilization, can one live without the 'me'? The monk says you can't—escape from the world, go to a monastery, change your name, devote your life to this or that, but the 'me' is still there because that 'me' has identified itself with the image it has projected of itself as this, that, or the other. The 'me' is still there in a different form.

So can one live—this is a tremendously important and very serious question—can one live without that 'me' in this monstrous world? That means can one live sanely in a world of insanity? It is insane, with all the make-believe of religions. Can you live in a world that is insane and yourself be totally sane?

Now who will answer that question except yourself? That means you have to see that your consciousness, with all its content, is the consciousness of the world. That is not a statement; that is a reality, something tremendously real. The content of your consciousness makes up your consciousness. Without the content there is no consciousness. Your content now is fear, pleasure, everything that is going on in the world, the culture that is so exalted, so praised—such a marvellous culture with its wars, brutalities, injustice, starvation, hunger—we are of that consciousness. And if your consciousness undergoes radical change, that change affects the consciousness of the world, it actually does. Take any of the people who have brought about physical so-called revolution, Lenin, the French Revolution people. You may not approve of what they did, but they affected the consciousness of the world, like Hitler, Mussolini, Stalin, and all that gang.

Q: Like Christ.

K: Oh! All right, Christ. You see how you escape? You escape into your old traditions. You don't say, 'Look, *I* have got to change. My consciousness must undergo a radical transformation'. This is the central issue: can your consciousness undergo a radical change? It can undergo that only when the central fact is seen that the observer is the observed. When you see that, all conflict inwardly comes to an end. But where there is division between the observer and the observed, anger and not anger, then there is conflict. When the Arab and the Jew see that they are the same human beings, there is no need for conflict. So can you observe your conflict and see that it is not separate from you, that you are that conflict?

Ojai, 13 April 1975

THE PROBLEM IS: what is action that is not always based on memory? Because action based on memory must inevitably lead to degeneracy. That is our problem. Because the human mind is degenerating, and one of the factors of that degeneration is conflict, fear, and the everlasting pursuit of pleasure, all based on the movement of thought that is a material process. Is there an action that is not degenerate? Is there an action that is perception and action? Actually perceiving and acting without the interval of time.

Let me put it another way. Life is relationship. Without relationship there is no life, living. Yet in one's relationship there is a great deal of accumulated memory; between two people there are hurts, nagging, pleasures, annoyances, domination, and so on. You know what happens in relationship. All that is stored up in memory as an image. You have an image about her, and she has an image about you. And these two images say, 'We are related. We love each other'. See what is happening: love is reduced to the images that you have about each other. Those images are memories, and so you call love a remembrance of things past. That is a fact; that happens in daily life. Now, can you live without these images? Only then is there love. In that relationship in which there is no image, there is an action from moment to moment that is always fresh.

You are related to somebody intimately, your wife, your girl, your boy, or whoever it is. Living together for a day or for fifteen or thirty years, you have created, put together an image about her or him. That is a fact. You can see it in your own life. That accumulation of various incidents, insults, annoyances, impatience, anger, pleasure, domination has become a memory, an image, and that image is always responding. That memory is always responding in the relationship. Now, can you live without building an image at all? Then only is there relationship. Now, can you do it, never create an image, whatever happens? Don't say yes or no; you are going to find out. If you say, 'No, it's not possible', then there is no problem; you go on in your own way. But if you want to find out, which means how to live differently, you must ask this question, whether you can live without a single image. Do you want to find out? I will point it out to you, and we will go together. I am not your guru, thank God, or your teacher or explainer—nothing.

You have to find out what is attention and what is inattention. I am related to you, intimately, family, and I have an image about you. Why has that image come into being at all? Does the image come into being when there is attention? So I must find out what attention is.

What is attention? Is attention concentration? What is concentration? When you concentrate, you exclude; you are putting your whole being on a certain point when you concentrate. Therefore you build a resistance around yourself, and in that resistance there is conflict, not wanting and wanting. So I must find out what attention is. If there is attention, will there be any image? Because relationship is of the highest importance in life. If I have right relationship with you, I have right relationship with everything, with nature, with my neighbour, with everything in life. And because I do not have right relationship with you, everything goes wrong. So I must find out, when there is attention, will there be an image? Or is there only an image when there is inattention? You understand my question? You say something cruel to me because you are my wife or husband or whatever. Because I am not paying attention, it is registered. But if I pay attention completely, at the moment of insult, do I register at all? Find out. Go into it and do it. That is, when there is attention, there is no centre. When you concentrate, there is a centre. When you are attending completely, there is no me, image, nothing. If, for instance, you are listening now with complete attention, if you are, what takes place? There is neither agreeing nor disagreeing; there is care, affection, love, so you are listening completely. In the same way, when in relationship there is a word, a gesture, a look that hurts, if at that moment there is complete attention, there is no image, nothing to register.

Saanen, 30 July 1978

WHAT DO WE mean by the word *order?* When you hear that word, what is your feeling, response, your instinctual answer? Order, according to the totalitarians, is to obey the few and conform to a pattern they have established. I am putting it in simplistic terms, but that's good enough to understand what they mean by the word *order.* There will be no dissent; we all think alike; we all work for the state. Anybody who deviates is called dissident and destroyed. That's one kind of order. We are going to question it.

Then there has been Victorian order—using the word *Victorian* in the sense of about the end of the nineteenth century—which meant keep everything outside orderly. Inwardly you might have chaos, mess, misery, but outwardly show that you are very orderly. In opposition to that we have more recently cultivated permissiveness. To the man or woman who is living in the permissive society, order is abomination. To the man or the woman who lived in the Victorian era, order was control, don't express your emotions, hold back, restrain. And now you have the totalitarian order. These are very simple facts, daily facts. Outwardly we say we must have order, and inwardly we are very disorderly. Would you say that? Disorderly means contradiction, confusion, giving importance to one thing in opposition to others, sex becoming enormously important, perhaps the only important thing, and the rest you put aside or delegate to second place. And inwardly there are constant struggle and battle—all that is disorder. This is clear, surely.

Now, what makes for disorder, both outwardly and inwardly? Are we aware that we live in disorder? Outwardly there is disorder when there is war. That is total organized terrorism blessed by the priests and respectable. Such total terrorism is obviously disorder, but it is respectable disorder, recognized by every human being as something necessary. There is disorder when there are nationalities. So outwardly there is disorder, and inwardly there is disorder. Are we familiar with our disorder inwardly? We know, when we read the newspapers and magazines, that there is this monstrous outward disorder. But it is much more arduous to be acquainted with our inward disorder. Now I am asking myself, and you are asking, what is the root of this disorder, why do we live this way? Why do we live like this? Why do we tolerate it? Why do we accept it? There is disorder between man and woman. However intimate, pleasant, comforting, and satisfying their relationship, there is constant struggle between man and woman, which is disorder.

Questioner: It isn't always so.

Krishnamurti: There may be exceptions, granted. One or two, half a dozen, a few people in the world may have a marvellous relationship with each other, but an appalling frightening relationship with the world. I said, may have.

So are we first of all familiar with this? Are we inwardly aware, cognizant? Do we see or observe that we live in disorder? There may be exceptions, that lady and a few others. If we are not aware that we live in disorder, who is going to tell you that you are? Nobody cares. On the contrary, they want you to live in disorder; it is profitable for society, for business, that you live in disorder because the moment you have order in yourself you become a danger.

So please find out for yourself whether, inwardly, your way of life is orderly or disorderly. Orderly may mean conforming to a pattern, conforming to a tradition. That is generally called orderly. Conforming to what the religious people have said—the monks, the gurus, the teachers, the so-called sacred books—if you follow and conform to those, you say, 'I am living in an orderly way'. Does conformity bring about order? Or is it the very root of disorder? One conforms when one puts on trousers and a shirt in this country; when one goes to India, one puts on different clothes. But we are talking of inward, psychological conformity. Do we conform? Does one know, realize that one is conforming?

❖

WE WILL GO more deeply into it. Begin with this: am I or are you conforming to a pattern, whether established by society or one I have established for myself? I may reject outward authority altogether, but inwardly I have the authority of my experience, of my knowledge, and to that I conform. And that is also conformity. So are you aware of this fact for yourself? If you are not, then who is going to awaken you? Who is going to put pressure on you so that you say, 'Yes, I am in disorder, I have found out'. Because through pressure you won't find out. It is pressure from outside that makes you conform or not conform. So if one may ask again, are you asking yourself, are you psychologically conforming in any way? This is one of the most subtle and important points if you go into it very deeply. You have to conform to certain laws; you have to drive on the right side in Europe and in England on the left side. If you say, 'Well, I am not going to conform', and drive on the right side, the police in England will be after you.

So please ask yourself whether you are conforming to tradition, to your aggressive, violent responses. Are you conforming to all that? You see what a tremendous problem this is. Whether you are imitating, not outwardly but inwardly, psychologically imitating. Will you take time, one afternoon, one evening, or some time during the day, to look at yourself? This is what you are doing now: you are, if I may most respectfully point out, looking at yourself and discovering for yourself whether you are conforming, imitating, whether you are conforming to one pattern, another conforming to another pattern, so there is conflict between the two and hence disorder.

Then if you know, realize, see that you are in disorder, will you remain with it—not try to change it, not try to say, 'I must go beyond, suppress, understand, rationalize it', but just hold it in your arms, as it were, without any movement? The baby is asleep in your arms; the moment you move, it wakes up and cries.

This is the point: will one comprehend and bring about order in one's life by rules, discipline, control, suppression; or will you observe in yourself disorder and not run away from it, not translate it into your own idiosyncrasies, temperament, but merely look at it, observe, watch it?

We have said on another occasion that the word *art* means to put things in their proper place, not giving one or the other undue importance. If you give too much importance to technology, then other ways of existence are given too little; therefore there is disharmony. If you give sex the highest, all-consuming importance, make it the only thing that matters in life, as most people do—perhaps there are exceptions—then again you exaggerate and bring about disharmony. If you rate money as all important, again contradiction takes place—or if you say power, domination is all important, again contradiction occurs. To live harmoniously, therefore means to put everything in its proper place. Will you do this—not give your body the tremendous importance the West gives it, how you look, how you dress—which doesn't mean you mustn't dress properly, decently. Will you do all this? If you don't, why do you talk about order? There is no point at all. But if one wants to live in order and therefore in harmony with a sense of great beauty, perhaps also peace, then you must have order.

Order has nothing to do with window-shopping! Never buying anything but going from shop to shop, and you think that is extraordinarily broad-minded, going from one book to another, one teacher to another, one guru to another, one priest to another, one philosopher to another. *Never, never, never staying in one place and finding out.* Why do people do that? Have you ever wondered? They go to India; they are fed up with their priest here, so perhaps there is someone there. That is all romantic nonsense. This is called gathering knowledge or having an open mind. It isn't really an open mind; it is a big sieve with large holes, with nothing but holes in it! We are doing this all the time in different ways. So we are asking, are you serious, committed, dedicated enough, to live a life of total order?

Q: It seems easier to live in disorder.

K: It is much easier to live in disorder—is it?

Q: They have not realized at all what disorder is if they like to live in disorder.

K: Please, let's find out for ourselves if we like to live in disorder—apparently most people do—disorder in their room, and so on; if we like it, there is nothing to be said about it. But if you say that living in disorder brings about havoc in one's life, misery, confusion, violence, then obviously you must know, become familiar with, your disorder.

If you find that you live in disorder, to find out what to do or what not to do, one has to go into the question: what is the very root of disorder that produces all this confusion, conflict, misery? Total disorder in the way we live—what is the root of it? Don't say, 'It's me', or 'the ego'—those are words—or thoughts. But find out for yourself.

Q: We accept the terror of the majority . . .

K: Sir, throw all that out. Throw out Krishnamurti and all that nonsense and find out for yourself. I am really not interested in myself. I am too old for all that kind of childish stuff.

Q: That we do not care for others is the source of disorder.

K: We are talking about disorder. What is the reason, the source, the essence of disorder? Just a minute, don't quote anybody, including myself. Because if you do you are just answering, saying something that others have said. So throw out what others have said, including this person. Don't belong to Krishnamurti. That would be fatal. Don't form Krishnamurti groups, for God's sake.

What is the root of disorder? Anything that is limited, that functions within a very narrow space must create disorder. If I love you as one human being and hate others, if I am attached to you and I don't care for the world at all as long as you and I are perfectly happy in our little home, it must create disorder. So we are discovering something: anything that acts, lives in a very small space, a very small shell, or even an enormous shell is still limited. Anything that moves, functions, and acts within a narrow space must create disorder. If I belong to that guru and not to any other gurus, then I am acting very limitedly. Obviously. But if I have no gurus at all, I don't follow anybody at all, then I may act widely.

So I am asking you: is disorder brought about by a limited way of life? My husband and nobody else. I say I must be kind, generous, compassionate, I must love others—but these are just words, because my whole centre is round one person or one thing. That may bring about disorder. So I have found that any action that is limited must create disorder. That is, if I act as a nationalist, it is disorder; if I act as a Catholic, Protestant, Hindu, Buddhist, all the rest of it, it is disorder.

Now have you looked at yourself, become familiar with yourself, and said, 'That is how it is. I will drop it, finished'? If you are interested in finding out what is order, then everything that creates disorder is dropped away instantly. Like a scientist doing research, which is the central thing he is concerned with, he is giving his whole life to it; other things are secondary. So can you find out for yourself if you are acting, living in a small circle?

Q: Do you think it is so easy to change oneself, to have an insight—there is disorder, and this is the reason?

K: Is it so easy to change oneself? That is the central question. I say yes. Don't *believe* it, because you are not going to change so easily. If you see real danger, as you see the danger of a precipice, you act. But you don't see the danger of limited action, a limited way of living. Which is I am attached to you, you are mine, and for God's sake let's live together peacefully, don't let's quarrel, and let's forget the world—the world is ugly. I have to go out into the world and earn money and all the rest of it, but we two are together. This becomes too childish.

❖

WHEN YOU UNDERSTAND the danger of disorder in life, which is expressed in different ways—conformity, living in a narrow little groove, or it may be very wide but it is still a groove if you see all that, not verbally, intellectually, but actually see the danger of it, it is finished. There is order.

Q: I think it is not so easy to change oneself. I have the insight now, I realize the dangers, then I go back to the city, back to my friends, and I forget it.

K: The city, business, the wife, the husband, are the most dangerous things because all that involves attachment. Wait a minute. It doesn't mean you can't be married and have a girlfriend and all the rest of it, but please see the danger of living as we are in a narrow little circle. You know in Saanen, this little village, they speak German. You go two miles away, they speak French, and people won't meet each other; they keep themselves in a very small circle. Now we are doing the same. Do you actually see the danger of that way of living? If you don't see it, how is one going to make you see it, help you to see it? Say I don't see the danger of conformity to a tradition, to a pattern, whether external or inward; I don't see that causes disorder. You have explained to me in ten different ways, but I refuse to see it. You understand? Because it is very disturbing, and I am used to living in a disorderly way, and your asking me to look at it frightens me. I am appalled by it.

You have got used to disorder; you have got used to wars; you have got used to quarrelling with your wife and husband. You have got used to living in this chaos. You know, this is very interesting: the word *cosmos* means order, and the universe is in order, complete order. And we live in disorder and try to understand cosmos, the universe. How can I understand something that is total order, without a break in it, when I myself am living in disorder?

Bombay, 31 January 1981

WHAT IS IT each of you wants? I can't give you money, a job, lead you to heaven, to salvation, so what can the speaker do? All he can do is point out certain factors, incidents, experiences that are detrimental to human existence; he can point out that nationalism is a great danger, communalism is a great danger, a small community opposed to global existence is a great danger, that any religion that does not liberate man is an extraordinary danger—your books, socalled sacred books, are worthless if they don't help you to be free. So can we together help each other to be free—free from fear, sorrow, anxiety so that we have some kind of peace, of love in the world? Can we do this together? Or is this impossible? Would you like the speaker to talk about the ending of sorrow? Would you like the speaker to convey to you a way of living that is totally different from the way we are living now? Is it possible that we can together bring about a totally different society? That will be possible only if our relationships are correct, if our actions are right.

Shall we go into the question of what is right action? Action that will be right under all circumstances, wherever you live, whatever the environment, however limited your activity—can we find out together what right action is? That is very important. So let's find out together the meaning of those two words, *right* and *action*. When we use the word *right*, it means whole, not fragmented, not broken up, an action that is complete, in which there are no regrets, that does not bring with it any kind of disturbance. Right means a movement that is constantly whole, precise, accurate under all circumstances. And action means doing—doing—not having done or will do. So right action means doing, means action that is whole, immediate. What is our actual action now? It is based on an ideal, a memory or an action that you *should* do, so our action is always building, always becoming. If we have a motive for an action, that action is essentially inaction, because in that action you are continually becoming, and you are therefore concerned only with becoming, not with action. So we are going to find out now for ourselves what right action is.

If you can really understand this for yourselves, you will have solved numerous problems. Our whole life is a becoming. If you are a clerk, you want to become a manager; if a manager, top manager; and so on. You want to climb the ladder, whether in business or in politics, and it is the same thing in the religious world. In the religious world if you are practising, following certain dicta, certain concepts, ideas, you are again becoming, constantly achieving. So our life is actually, if you observe it, a constant process of becoming. In that becoming time is involved. I am this, I will be that, which means a movement from here to there, a psychological distance. You need time to go from here to your home. There, it is necessary because you live far away or near. Whether you live far away or near, that involves time. Psychologically, inwardly, you say to yourself, I am this, but I will become that. There is a distance between what you are and what you want to be, which is time in which you are becoming something. So our life is always a becoming, and in that becoming there is action. Right? So action is never complete. I wonder if you see this. When you are allowing time in action, that time indicates that you are moving from one point to another point. So your action will inevitably be limited, and therefore any action that is limited will bring about greater conflict.

So is there an action that does not involve time? Please see the importance of this. There is biological time, growth from the infant, there is psychological time, and there is time by the watch, which is day and night. So there are three types of time: biological time, you can't do anything about that, but time is involved in the very genes. In order to grow from childhood to manhood, old age, time is necessary there. And time is necessary to go from here to your house. But we also think time is necessary for bringing about right action: I will learn what right action is, and that learning implies time. So is there an action that does not involve time, which means, is there an action that is not controlled by the idea of becoming? Is that all right? Please see the importance of what is involved in time, psychological time. That is, I am angry; I will take time to get over my anger. That is how our brain functions; it has been trained through millennia to function that way. You also think that illumination or enlightenment needs time, life after life, following a system of meditation, obeying, that all that involves time.

We are saying time is danger. Psychological time is danger because it prevents you from acting. If you are violent, if you say, 'I will be non-violent', you have taken time. In that time you are not free from violence; you are being violent. So if you understand the nature of time, there will be immediate action. That is, there is the ending of violence immediately. Let us understand the question of time. It is very important because we think we need time to change; we think we need time to grow, to evolve—that time means that, that is, what we are and what we should be. This is our constant, continuous tradition, our conditioning. Now we are pointing out the *danger* of psychological time, not biological time or time by the watch, but psychological time, that is, admitting tomorrow, a tomorrow that may be a hundred days away, but the idea that time is necessary to change from 'what is' to 'what should be'. So we are saying that is one of the most dangerous factors in life, to admit time in action. Now wait a minute. I need time to learn a language; I need time to take an engineering degree. If I want to be a computer expert, I have to study, go into it, take time; it takes time to go from here to your house. We need time physically to go from here to over there. We need time to learn a language; we need time to become an expert in anything; to be a good carpenter, you need time for all that.

So our whole brain is working with the concept of time. Our whole way of life is to become something. And this becoming is the most dangerous factor in action. You see, we have never inquired whether it is possible not to have tomorrow, not to have a future; the future is the becoming. Also, we have never inquired into what is being. We have accepted the tradition, the conditioning, that all life is becoming. You plant a seed; it becomes a plant, a tree; that takes time. So that same movement is accepted in the psychological world. We are questioning that. We are saying any form of psychological becoming not only prevents actual action but is an illusion. *There is no psychological tomorrow,* but thought has created the idea of becoming, and thought has projected the tomorrow—not that there is no tomorrow; there is, you have got to get up tomorrow—the idea that psychologically, inwardly, I will become something; I will ultimately find heaven; I will find enlightenment; life after life, if I live rightly, I will have my reward. Time is necessary for a plant to grow, and we also think time is necessary to become something.

Now, in that becoming lie all our problems: I must be better, more loving, or I am greedy for money, and I keep pursuing money, money, money. So you see what is happening? The brain is the result of time; it has evolved from the ape to the present time; it has grown through experience, knowledge, memory, thought, and action. Now see what is happening? Experience, knowledge, memory, action—to acquire knowledge requires time.

So we are asking, what is right action? It cannot be in the field of time. I can't learn about right action. If I learn about right action, that learning takes time. If you catch the full meaning of this immediately, then out of that immediate perception *is* action that is not involved in time. I will go into this more deeply.

As the speaker said, time is danger. Either you perceive directly and act directly now, or you say, 'I will think over what you have said and see if you are right or wrong'. Then you are taking time, whereas if you say, 'Let me listen very carefully to what he is saying', this means you are paying attention, and that attention has no time. You attend, you listen, not you will listen or you listen and interpret what is being said, which takes time, or you translate what you hear into what you already know, which also takes time. So can you listen so completely that you catch immediately the significance of time? I will go into it again. Scientists, especially the computer experts, have realized that what thought can do or has done, the computer can do. That is a fact. What thought can do, the computer can do much faster, much more accurately; it can do extraordinary things. They are asking, what, then, is intelligence? If the computer can do what thought can do, what is man? Now the computer is programmed by a human being, and the computer can never be free from knowledge; it is based on knowledge. Human beings can be free from knowledge. That is the only difference. The freeing from knowledge is not time.

Man is the only one who can free himself from the known. The computer can't. The known is time; to acquire knowledge needs time. Wait, to know oneself, you think you need time. To know myself is to read the book of mankind. I am mankind, and I think I need time to read that book. I have to understand why I have reactions, why I have accumulated memory, why this and that. So to read that book, which is self-knowledge, we think we need time. That is, I need to know myself, which is the whole structure of knowledge. To know myself, I think I need time. We are applying the same principle for learning a language to learning about myself or about you. So we think time is necessary. *And I don't need time there.* We think we need time to become.

So we are asking, does right action imply time? I am going to show you something. Our actions are based on experience, knowledge, memory, thought. That is the chain in which we live, from which we act. That process is a movement in time. Now we are pointing out something else, which is that this movement of knowledge, experience, memory, action, and then repeating that same pattern is time, and as we have lived in that process we are caught, conditioned by it. Now, to act means the doing now, not tomorrow, not to have acted. Action means doing, the doing without time. That is action. So if you have a problem, not to carry that problem overnight, not to allow time to solve it; time will never solve it. Not to burden your mind with psychological problems. If you are a technician, you have been trained to solve problems. That is simple. But now you are being conditioned by time, that is, acquiring knowledge and acting from knowledge, acting from that which you have learned. We are saying see this movement—experience, knowledge, memory, thought, action—see that fact. That is a fact; see it in the sense, be aware of it, and if you see that very clearly, your perception then is without time and therefore action in which time is not involved at all. I will show you.

Most people are hurt psychologically from childhood. In school, you are compared with somebody else who is brighter, and you get hurt. This hurt is carried through school, college, university, or you get hurt psychologically, inwardly, in some other way by somebody, by a word, a gesture, a look. We are all of us, most human beings, psychologically hurt. *What is hurt is the image that you have built about yourself.* That is clear. That *image* is hurt. As long as you have an image, you are going to be hurt, or flattered—it is the same thing, two sides of the same coin. That's a fact. Most human beings are hurt—they carry it throughout life—and that hurt results in more and more withdrawal, fear, resistance, avoidance, isolation. You see all that. That is, you have listened; you see the reasons, see the logic of it; you have comprehended it intellectually, which means you have understood only the verbal meaning but don't actually see the truth of it. The truth is that as long as you are hurt, that hurt is the image you have about yourself created by your society, family, education, and so on. You have built that image like the politician who builds an image about himself, wanting power, position, and when somebody comes along and puts a pin in your image, you get hurt. Now, do you see that fact, or is it merely an idea? You understand the difference?

You hear verbally what is being said. You listen to it and then make an abstraction of it that becomes an idea that you then pursue and not the actuality. Do you see the actual fact that you have an image about yourself? If you do, and that is a fact, that image is going to be hurt. You can't escape from it. It is there. Now do you completely realize that as long as you have an image about yourself, you are going to be hurt? Do you see that as a fact? If you see that as a fact, then you can inquire who created it. Thought, experience, education, family, tradition, all that goes to create the image. And you see the truth that as long as you have an image you are going to be hurt with all its consequences. If you see that, perceive the actual fact, then the image disappears instantly. If you say, "How am I to get rid of the image? Show me the method, I will practise it", in all that you are allowing time, and therefore you are perpetuating the image. Whereas if you see the fact, the truth that as long as you have an image about anything, you are going to be hurt, the seeing of the truth is the ending of the image. That is, seeing the fact is all important. Perception and immediate action.

So we human beings have problems. As I said, one of these problems is conflict, conflict between 'what is' and 'what should be'. That is a conflict. And belief in any form, which gives a certain kind of psychological security, is detrimental to man. If you see conflict is a danger, look at it, see all the consequences of it, see it as a fact, and don't move away from that fact, then the very perception of it is the ending of it. That is why one has to understand the enormous complexity of time. If you understand it intellectually, it has no value; it's just a verbal communication. But if you really understand, that is, see actually that you are greedy—and do not say, I must not be greedy, then you are wandering away from it—if you stay with greed, see it instantly, that very perception is the action that ends it. Are you *doing* it, or are you just *verbally* accepting all this?

As we said, we have been exploring together our human brain, our human life, everyday life with all its conflicts, illusions, and so on. And we think time, the next life, will solve all these problems. Time is the greatest enemy you can possibly have, because time prevents action, action that is whole, complete, undivided so that it does not leave a mark as regret. So if you have listened very carefully, seen it for yourself, you will understand that freedom from time is the greatest enlightenment.

Ojai, 2 May 1982

TOGETHER WE ARE observing why human beings cannot live at peace with each other. That is a statement of fact, not exaggerated; and our approach to it is either with pure, non-personal, objective observation or with a personal reaction. If you approach it with a personal reaction, conflict will go on forever. But if you approach it objectively, dispassionately, without any direction—what is the state of your mind when looking at the problem? All right, let's put it another way. Why is there conflict between man and woman, man and man, you know, the whole area of relationship? Look at it please; answer it yourself, go into it yourself; don't depend on me, on the speaker—that has no value. He is just a verbal entity, a telephone. *You* have to find out why. We are observing together. You are not learning from the speaker; he is not teaching you anything. You are not his followers; he is not your authority; he is not your guru.

In observing together, we are going to discover why this conflict exists, whether it is possible to end it completely; not theoretically, not for a day, but end it. This conflict exists, must exist because—I don't want to tell you, because it becomes so silly. If I tell you, you'll say, yes, that's quite right; and then you are back. It isn't something that you yourself have discovered. Do you know what happens when you discover something for yourself psychologically? You have immense energy, and you need that to free the mind of its conditioning. I quarrel with my wife, if I have one, or a girlfriend, whoever it is—quarrel with her because I am a lonely man, I want to possess her. I want to depend on her; I want her comfort, her encouragement, her companionship, somebody to tell me I'm marvellous. So I am building an image about her; and she also wants to be possessed, wants sexual fulfilment in me, wants me to be something different from what I am. Each one living together maybe for a day, a week, or years has built an image that becomes knowledge, knowledge about each other.

May I go into the question of knowledge a little? This is serious. Knowledge is destructive in relationship. I say I know my wife because I have lived with her, I know all her tendencies, irritations, impetuosity, jealousy, which becomes my knowledge about her: how she walks, how she does her hair, how she moves. I have collected a lot of information and knowledge about her. And she has collected a lot of knowledge about me, from the past—knowledge is always the past—there is no knowledge about the future. So we have this knowledge about each other.

We then have to inquire a great deal into the question of knowledge: what place has knowledge in life? Are we together in this observation? Will knowledge transform man? What place has knowledge in the mutation or ending of conditioning? This is conditioning; I have conditioned her through knowledge, and she has conditioned me through knowledge. Please, I am not teaching you. You are observing with all your energy, capacity to see this fact: that where there is knowledge in relationship, there must be conflict. I must have knowledge to drive a car, to write a sentence, to speak English or French. I must have technological knowledge. If I am a good carpenter, I must have knowledge about the wood, the tools I use, and so on; but in relationship with my wife, with a friend, whoever it is, that knowledge I have gathered, put together through constant irritation, constant separation, ambition, is going to prevent actual relationship.

Is this a fact, or merely a supposition, a theory, an idea? An idea is an abstraction from a fact. The Greek word *idea* means to observe, to see, to come very close to perception, not make an abstraction that becomes an idea. So we are not dealing with ideas but with the actual relationship, which is in conflict, and that conflict arises when I have accumulated a lot of information about her and she has acquired a lot about me. So our relationship then is based on knowledge, and knowledge can never be complete about anything in life. Please realize this. Knowledge must always go with the shadow of ignorance. You can't know about the universe. Astrophysicists may describe it, but to be aware of that immensity, no knowledge is required through information; you have to have a mind that is as vast, as completely orderly as the universe is. That's a different matter.

❖

SO IT IS very important to understand the place of knowledge and of knowledge as an impediment in relationship. Love is not knowledge; love is not remembrance. When there is no knowledge about her, I look on her as a fresh, new human being, each day new. Do you know what that does? You are too learned, full of book knowledge, what other people have said. That's why a very simple thing like this becomes awfully difficult to comprehend.

Bombay, 23 January 1983

THIS GLORIFIED TRIBALISM called nationalism has brought about a great many wars; and where there is division, not only division in the relationship between man and woman, but also racial, religious, and linguistic divisions, there must be conflict. We went into the question: why does this constant conflict exist? What is the root of it, the cause of all this chaos, almost anarchy, the bad governments, arming different groups, each nation preparing for war, thinking one religion is superior to the other? We see this division throughout the world, and it has existed historically for many centuries. What is the cause? Who is responsible for it? We said it is thought that has divided man against man—thought, which has also created extraordinary architecture, painting, poetry, and the whole world of technology, medicine, surgery, communications, computers, robots, and so on. Thought has brought about good health, good medicine, various forms of human comfort.

But thought has also created this vast division between man and man, and so we ask: what is the cause of all this? We said where there is a cause, there is an end to it; when you have a certain disease, the cause can be found and the disease cured. Wherever there is a cause, there is an end to that cause. That is obviously a fact. And if thought has created this confusion, uncertainty, this perpetual danger of war, if thought is responsible for that, then what is to happen if thought is not to be used in this way?

We also said that this is not a lecture. We are investigating, exploring together to find out why man—woman of course included—perpetuates conflict throughout the world not only within himself but outwardly—in society, in religion, in the economy. If thought is responsible, which is fairly obvious, for the mess, the division, all the misery of human beings, if one recognizes that as a fact, not as a theory or philosophical statement, but if one realizes the actual fact that however clever, crafty, erudite it is, thought is responsible, then what is man to do?

We have also said that thought has created marvellous cathedrals, temples, and mosques, and that everything they contain is the invention of thought. Thought has created God. Because thought finds uncertainty, insecurity, conflict in this world, thought seeks, invents an entity, a principle, an ideal that gives security, comfort, but that comfort and security are its own invention. I think it is fairly obvious, if you observe your own thinking, that thought, however subtle or stupid, cunning, crafty, has created this division and conflict. Then we can ask, why does this conflict exist? Why have we lived from time immemorial with this conflict between good and bad, the 'what is' and 'what should be', the actual and the ideal?

Let us inquire not only why there is conflict but also why there is division as good and bad, as evil and that which is beautiful, holy. Please, we are thinking together, not agreeing, not accepting, but having observed the state of the world, the society in which you live, your own governments, economic situation, and the various gurus, when you have observed all this objectively, rationally, sanely, why does man live in conflict? What is conflict? If I may remind you—I shall over and over again—we are having a dialogue together. You and the speaker are having a conversation, not just listening to some ideas, concepts, or words, but you are sharing. You can only share, partake, if you are really concerned.

If we merely treat what is being said as a series of ideas, conclusions, suppositions, then our dialogue ends; there is no communication between you and the speaker. But there is if you are concerned, at all awake to all the things that are happening in the world—the tyranny, the search for power, accepting power, living with power. All power is evil, ugly, whether power over the wife or the wife over the husband or the power of governments throughout the world. Where there is power, it goes with all the ugly things.

So we are asking why man lives in conflict. Not only between two people, man and woman, but also one community against another community, one group against another group. What is the nature of conflict? We are talking about very serious things, not philosophy, but investigating the life that we lead day after day, year after year till we die. Why do human beings live with conflict? Some of you may have seen those caves in the south of France from twenty-five, thirty thousand years ago; there is a picture of a man fighting evil in the form of a bull. For thousands of years we have lived with conflict. To meditate becomes a conflict. Everything that we do or don't do has become a conflict.

Does conflict exist where there is comparison? Comparison means measurement; one compares oneself with another who may be bright, intelligent, a man with a position, power and so on. Where there is comparison, there must be fear, there must be conflict. So can one live without comparison at all? We think by comparing ourselves with somebody we are progressing. You want to be like your guru or beat your guru, go beyond him. You want to achieve enlightenment, status; you want a following; you want to be respected. Where there is a becoming psychologically, there must be conflict. Are we together thinking about this? Whether it is possible to live a life, a modern life, without any comparison and therefore without any conflict? We are questioning psychological becoming. A child becomes an adult, then grows into manhood. To learn a language, we need time; to acquire any skill, we need time. And we are asking: is psychological becoming one of the reasons of conflict? I want 'what is' to be changed into 'what should be'. I am not good, but I will be good. I am greedy, envious, but perhaps one day I will be free of all that.

The desire to become, which is measurement, comparison, is that one of the causes of conflict? Is there another reason? Is there duality? This is not philosophy. We are examining something to understand the nature of conflict and find out for ourselves if it is possible to be completely free of conflict. Conflict wears out the brain, makes the mind old. A man who has lived without conflict is an extraordinary human being. Tremendous energy is dissipated in conflict. So it is important, if one may point out, necessary, to understand conflict. Now we have seen that measurement, comparison, brings about conflict.

Also, we have stated that there is duality. Some of your philosophers have posited that and have said that this is one of the reasons for conflict. There is duality—night and morning, light and shade, tall and short, bright and dull, sun rising and sun setting. Physically there is duality. You are a woman, and he is a man. Please think together with the speaker, not accepting what he says, because then we can co-operate together. That means you must put aside your opinions, conclusions, and experiences, because if you stick to them and another also sticks to his, then there is no co-operation, no thinking together. There is division; there is conflict. So I beg of you, let us think together, because this is very serious. Is there psychological duality at all? Or is there only 'what is'? I am violent. That's the only state—violence—not non-violence. Non-violence is just an idea; it is not a fact. So where there are violence and non-violence, there must be conflict. In this country you have talked endlessly about non-violence, but probably you are also very violent people. So the fact and the non-fact: the fact is human beings throughout the world are violent. That is a fact. Violence means not only physical violence but also imitation, conformity, obedience, acceptance.

Fact is 'what is'; the other is not. But if you are conditioned to the other, that is, you pursue, while violent, non-violence, you move away from the fact, and then you must have conflict. Because while I am seeking non-violence, I am being violent; I am sowing seeds of violence. There is only one fact, and that is I am violent. So in the understanding of the nature and structure of violence there may be the ending of violence.

So there is only fact, not the opposite. This is very clear—that the ideal, the principle, that which you call the noble, are all illusions. What is fact is that we are violent, ignoble, corrupt, uncertain, and so on. Those are facts, and we have to deal with facts. Facts, if you face them, do not create problems; that is how it is. So I discover that I am violent, and I have no opposite to it; I reject totally the opposite as meaningless. I have only this fact. How do I look at the fact? What is my motive in looking at it? What is the direction in which I want the fact to move? I must be aware of the nature and structure of the fact, be aware of it without choice. Are you doing this as we are talking? Or you are just happily listening to a lot of words and picking up here and there some that seem convenient and suitable and not listening totally to your own inquiry?

How does one deal with fact? How do I observe the fact that I am violent? That violence shows when I am angry, jealous, when I try to compare myself with another. If I am doing all that, then it is impossible to face facts. A good mind faces facts. If you are in business, you face facts and deal with them; you don't pretend you will achieve something by moving away from them. Then you are not a good businessman. But here we are so ineffectual, we don't change, because we don't deal with facts. Psychologically, inwardly we avoid them. We escape from them, or, when we do discover them, we suppress them. So there is no resolution of any of them.

From that we can go to something else, which is important. What is a good mind? Have you ever asked that? Is a mind good when it is full of knowledge? And what is knowledge? We are all very proud of having knowledge, scholastic knowledge, through experience, incidents, accidents. Knowledge is accumulated memory, accumulated experience, and experience can never be complete. So is a good mind full of knowledge? Is a good mind a free, comprehensive, global mind? Or is a good mind parochial, narrow, nationalistic, traditional? That is not a good mind, obviously. A good mind is a free mind. It is not a contemporary mind. A good mind is not of a time, not concerned with environment. It can deal with environment, deal with time. But in itself it is totally free. And such a mind has no fear. The speaker is saying this because our minds have been so educated, so trained that we have nothing original. There is no depth; knowledge is always superficial.

We are concerned with understanding the human being, his mind, action, behaviour, responses, which are limited because his senses are limited. To understand the depth, the nature of conflict and whether it is possible to be completely free of it, one must have a good mind, not just an accumulation of words. This does not mean a clever mind, a crafty mind, which most of us have. We have very crafty minds but not good minds. We are very cunning, subtle, deceptive, dishonest, but those are not the qualities of a good mind. So is it possible for us, living in this modern world, to have a good mind, with all the activities, pressures, influences, and newspapers and constant repetition—our minds are being programmed like a computer—if you have been programmed as a Hindu for the last three thousand years, you are repetitive. Such repetition is not the sign of a good mind—which is strong, healthy, active, decisive, full of passionate alertness. Such a mind is necessary. Only then is it possible to bring about a psychological revolution and thus a new society, a new culture.

The art of listening is to listen, see the truth, and act. For us, we see something to be true, we understand it logically, reasonably, but we don't act. There is an interval between perception and action. Between perception and action many other incidents take place; therefore you will never act. If you see violence in yourself as a fact and do not try to become non-violent, which is non-fact, you will see the nature, the complexity of violence; and you can see that if you listen to your own violence, it will reveal its nature. You can know it yourself. When you perceive your violence and act, then violence ends completely. Whereas perception with an interval before action is conflict.

From Krishnamurti to Himself, *Ojai, 31 March 1983*

MAN IS NOW posing a question he should have put to himself many years ago, not at the last moment. He has been preparing for wars all the days of his life. Preparation for war seems unfortunately to be our natural tendency. Having come a long way along that path, we are now saying: what shall we do? What are we human beings to do? Actually facing the issue, what is our responsibility? This is what is really facing our present humanity, not what kinds of instruments of war we should invent and build. We always bring about a crisis and then ask ourselves what to do. Given the situation as it is now, the politicians and the vast general public will decide with their national, racial pride, with their fatherlands and motherlands and all the rest of it.

The question is too late. The question we must put to ourselves, in spite of the immediate action to be taken, is whether it is possible to stop all wars, not a particular kind of war, the nuclear or the orthodox, and find out most earnestly what are the causes of war. Until those causes are discovered, dissolved, whether we have conventional war or the nuclear form of war, we will go on, and man will destroy man.

So we should really ask: what are essentially, fundamentally, the causes of war? See together the true causes, not invented, not romantic, patriotic causes and all that nonsense, but actually see why man prepares to murder legally—war. Until we research and find the answer, wars will go on. But we are not seriously enough considering, or committed to, the uncovering of the causes of war. Putting aside what we are now faced with, the immediacy of the issue, the present crisis, can we not together discover the true causes and put them aside, dissolve them? This needs the urge to find the truth.

Why is there, one must ask, this division—the Russian, the American, the British, the French, the German, and so on— why is there this division between man and man, between race and race, culture against culture, one series of ideologies against another? Why? Why is there this separation? Man has divided the earth as yours and mine—why? Is it that we try to find security, self-protection, in a particular group, or in a particular belief, faith? For religions also have divided man, put man against man—the Hindus, the Moslems, the Christians, the Jews, and so on. Nationalism, with its unfortunate patriotism, is really a glorified form, an ennobled form, of tribalism. In a small tribe or in a very large tribe there is a sense of being together, having the same language, the same superstitions, the same kind of political, religious system. And one feels safe, protected, happy, comforted. And for that safety, comfort, we are willing to kill others who have the same kind of desire to be safe, to feel protected, to belong to something. This terrible desire to identify oneself with a group, with a flag, with a religious ritual, and so on gives us the feeling that we have roots, that we are not homeless wanderers. There is the desire, the urge, to find one's roots.

And also we have divided the world into economic spheres, with all their problems. Perhaps one of the major causes of war is heavy industry. When industry and economics go hand in hand with politics, they must inevitably sustain a separative activity to maintain their economic stature. All countries are doing this, the great and the small. The small are being armed by the big nations—some quietly, surreptitiously, others openly. Is the cause of all this misery, suffering, and the enormous waste of money on armaments the visible sustenance of pride, of wanting to be superior to others?

It is our earth, not yours or mine or his. We are meant to live on it, helping each other, not destroying each other. This is not some romantic nonsense but the actual fact. But man has divided the earth, hoping thereby that in the particular he is going to find happiness, security, a sense of abiding comfort. Until a radical change takes place and we wipe out all nationalities, all ideologies, all religious divisions, and establish a global relationship psychologically first, inwardly before organizing the outer—we shall go on with wars. If you harm others, if you kill others, whether in anger or by organized murder, which is called war, you, who are the rest of humanity, not a separate human being fighting the rest of mankind, are destroying yourself.

This is the real issue, the basic issue, which you must understand and resolve. Until you are committed, dedicated, to eradicating this national, economic, religious division, you are perpetuating war. You are responsible for all wars, whether nuclear or traditional.

This is really a very important and urgent question: whether man, you, can bring about this change in yourself—not say, 'If I change, will it have any value? Won't it be just a drop in a vast lake and have no effect at all? What is the point of my changing?' That is a wrong question, if one may point out. It is wrong because you are the rest of mankind. You are the world; you are not separate from the world. You are not an American, Russian, Hindu, or Moslem. You are apart from these labels and words; you are the rest of mankind because your consciousness, your reactions, are similar to the others. You may speak a different language, have different customs. That is superficial culture—all cultures apparently are superficial—but your consciousness, your reactions, your faith, your beliefs, your ideologies, your fears, anxieties, loneliness, sorrow, and pleasure are similar to the rest of mankind. If you change, it will affect the whole of mankind.

This is important to consider—not vaguely, superficially—in inquiring into, researching, seeking out the causes of war. War can only be understood and put an end to if you and all those who are concerned very deeply with the survival of man feel that you are utterly responsible for killing others. What will make you change? What will make you realize the appalling situation that we have brought about now? What will make you turn your face against all division—religious, national, ethical, and so on? Will more suffering? But you have had thousands upon thousands of years of suffering, and man has not changed; he still pursues the same tradition, same tribalism, the same religious divisions of 'my God' and 'your God'.

The gods or their representatives are invented by thought; they have actually no reality in daily life. Most religions have said that to kill human beings is the greatest sin. Long before Christianity, the Hindus said this, the Buddhists said it, yet people kill in spite of their belief in God, or their belief in a saviour, and so on; they still pursue the path of killing. Will the reward of heaven change you, or the punishment of hell? That too has been offered to man. And that too has failed. No external imposition, laws, systems will ever stop the killing of man. Nor will any intellectual, romantic conviction stop wars. They will stop only when you, as the rest of humanity, see the truth that as long as there is division in any form, there must be conflict, limited or wide, narrow or expansive, that there must be struggle, conflict, pain. So you are responsible not only to your children but to the rest of humanity. Unless you deeply understand this, not verbally or ideationally or merely intellectually, but feel this in your blood, in your way of looking at life, in your actions, you are supporting organized murder, which is called war. The immediacy of perception is far more important than the immediacy of answering a question that is the outcome of a thousand years of man killing man.

The world is sick, and there is no one outside you to help you except yourself. We have had leaders, specialists, every kind of external agency, including God—they have had no effect; they have in no way influenced your psychological state. They cannot guide you. No statesman, no teacher, no guru, no one can make you strong inwardly, supremely healthy. As long as you are in disorder, as long as your house is not kept in a proper condition, a proper state, you will create the external prophet, and he will always be misleading you. Your house is in disorder, and no one on this earth or in heaven can bring about order in your house. Unless you yourself understand the nature of disorder, the nature of conflict, the nature of division, your house—that is, you—will always remain in disorder, at war.

It is not a question of who has the greatest military might, but rather it is man against man, man who has put together ideologies, and these ideologies, which man has made, are against each other. Until these ideas, ideologies, end and man becomes responsible for other human beings, there cannot possibly be peace in the world.

Saanen, 26 July 1983

Questioner: You said it is necessary to have no opinions about anything. I feel it is necessary to have opinions about such serious things as nazism, communism, the spread of armaments, the use of torture by governments. One can't just sit and observe these things taking place. Mustn't one say something or perhaps do something?

Krishnamurti: You are not going to catch me! I am not going to catch you, either! This is not a game we are playing. Why do we have opinions? I am not saying it is necessary or not necessary. Why do we have them? Opinions are something that has not been proved—prejudice is also a form of opinion. So why do we have them? Not that there are not nazism, the spreading of armaments, and the use of torture by governments. That is going on; every government is indulging in all that in the name of peace, law, patriotism, God. Every religion has tortured people except Buddhism and Hinduism. Now these are facts. Britain sells armaments to Argentina. See the ridiculousness of it. France and other countries sell armaments. You may have strong opinions that this should not happen. What are you going to do? Join a group, demonstrate, shout slogans, be beaten up by the police, have tear gas thrown at you? You have seen all that on television or experienced it if you are part of the circus, part of the show.

Has your opinion brought about a change? The armaments thing has been going on for centuries. They all say we must not do it, and yet big business, industry, says we can't exist if we don't. So will you stop paying taxes? If you do, you are sent to prison. First of all, see the logic of all this. What will you do about these things? They are all wrong, cruel; they bring about a great deal of violence. That is a fact. Chile is now torturing people; it happens in Belfast and so on. No government is free of it; whether it is done subtly or obviously, it is going on. Now what is one to do? You may be strongly opposed to nazism, Hitler, and company. They have done terrible things in the world. Germany was a highly civilized European country that excelled in philosophy, in inventions. That very great cultured people was taken over by a lunatic.

Now what is an opinion? I have an opinion against all this. What value has that opinion? Will it affect the selling of armaments, prevent nazism, prevent torture? Or is the whole thing much deeper than merely having opinions? There is a more serious, deeper question: why is man against man? Ask that question, not whether my opinion is justified or not. Why, after all these centuries of so-called civilization and culture, is man against man? If we could go into that, which requires much more serious inquiry than holding or not holding opinions, then we will enter into an area where we might do something.

Why are you, as a human being, against another human being? Against another ideology? You have your own ideology, but you are against another one. The democratic ideology and the totalitarian ideology are at war. Why do men live by ideologies? Ideologies are not real, are something that thought has invented. Thought, after a great deal of study of materialistic philosophy, comes to a certain conclusion, and that becomes a law for some people, and they want everyone else to accept it. The other side does much the same thing in a different way. The democratic world, so-called free world, doesn't put us in prison because we can sit here and talk. In a totalitarian state that would probably not be possible.

We are asking a much more fundamental, deeper question: why is man against man? Aren't you against somebody? Aren't you violent? And you are the whole of humanity. I know we like to think we are separate individuals, private souls—but we are not. You are the rest of mankind because you suffer, agonize, are lonely, depressed like all the rest. So you are basically, fundamentally the rest of mankind. You are humanity, and you are, whether you like it or not, in the global sense. If you are antagonistic, violent, aggressive, patriotic, my country is better than your country, my culture is the highest, and all that nonsense, then you are selling armaments; you have helped to torture people because you are a Catholic, a Protestant, a Hindu. Where there is division, there must be conflict and all the rest of it. So are you acting wholly, or is it the little me acting? Then you are a man against another.

Q: From what we read, you have had strange and mysterious experiences. Is this kundalini or something greater? We read that you consider the so-called process that you have undergone to be some sort of expansion of consciousness. Could it be instead self-induced and psychosomatic, caused by tension? Is not Krishnamurti's consciousness put together by thought and words?

K: Somebody is interested in this, so I must answer it. Are you interested in this? Of course. This is much more exciting than desire! I wish you would be simple about all this. Krishnamurti has apparently had various experiences. They may be psychosomatic, induced by tension, or a pleasurable projection of his own desires, and so on. In India the word *kundalini* has a great meaning. They have written books about it, and several people claim they have awakened it. I won't go into all that. Don't be mesmerised by this word. It means a kind of release of energy so that it is inexhaustible. It has other and different meanings—to awaken energy and to let it function completely. And the so-called process may be imagination and so on.

Do these things matter? They are experimenting in Russia with reading other people's thoughts. Andropov can read Mr. Reagan's thoughts, Mr. Reagan can read Mr. Andropov's thoughts, and then the game is up! If you can read my thoughts and I can read yours, then life becomes terribly complex and rather tiresome. They have experimented with this at Duke University in America. This is all the old Indian tradition. Perhaps Krishnamurti has done some of these things, but is this important? It is like having a good bath—after a hot day having a healthy bath with a clean towel and good soap, and at the end of it you are clean. What matters is that you are clean. Put all this at that level. Don't give this importance. Krishnamurti has been through all this; he knows a great deal about it. But he treats all this as unnecessary. There is energy that has been misused by us, in fights, quarrels, pretensions, trying to say mine is better than yours, I have reached this platform, and so on. It is far more important to inquire why human beings behave as they do now, not all this triviality. This *is* triviality. We have discussed it with some of the people who claim to have had this awakening. You have a little experience, and then you set up shop. Then I become a guru; then I am in business. I have disciples, I tell them what to do, I have money, I sit in a posture, and I am very . . . all that tommy-rot!

So one has to be terribly careful of one's own little experiences. What is really important is to find out sanely, rationally, logically how you waste your energy through conflict, quarrels, fear, and pretension. When all that energy is not being wasted, you have all the energy in the world. As long as your brain is not deteriorating through conflict, ambition, strife, fighting, loneliness, depression, and all the rest of it, you have an abundance of energy. But if you just release some kind of little energy, then you do an infinite harm to others.

So please don't fall into the trap of those gurus who say, 'I know; you don't know; I will tell you'. There are various centres in America and probably in Europe and India where one or two people are saying, 'I have awakened this peculiar stuff, and I will tell you all about it. I will teach you'. You know, the good old game! It all becomes so trivial when man is fighting man, the world is degenerating, disintegrating, and you are talking about footling little experiences.

Also, the questioner asks: is not Krishnamurti's consciousness put together by thought, as every consciousness with its content is the result of the movement of thought? Your consciousness has its content of fear, belief, loneliness, anxiety, sorrow, following somebody, having faith, saying my country is better, the highest culture. All that is part of your consciousness; it is what you are. If you are free of that, then you are in a totally different dimension. That is not expansion of consciousness; it is denying the content of consciousness, not expanding and becoming more and more self-centred.

San Francisco, 5 May 1984

To inquire into and observe the whole psychological world of each one of us, you require passion, not just intellectual entertainment, dissection, or analysis. You need passion and energy. That energy is now being wasted through conflict, because each of us, whether rich or poor, ignorant or a great scientist, the ordinary person with a monotonous daily life or the uneducated man in the small jungle village, lives in constant conflict. All human beings have great conflict, struggle, pain. To inquire whether it is possible to end that inward, psychological conflict demands not only energy but real passion: passion to find out whether human conflict can ever end or must go on everlastingly.

According to the archaeologists and biologists, we are supposed to have lived on this earth for some forty to fifty thousand years—from the most ancient civilizations to the present time. We have all lived in conflict, not only with nature but also inwardly and externally through wars. This duration of forty or fifty thousand years of human evolution has brought us to where we are now—still in conflict. I wonder if we realize that, not theoretically, not intellectually, but actually realize how deeply we are in conflict with each other, and not only with each other but in ourselves. We have accepted conflict as our way of life, externally as war, which is the glorification of tribalism, destroying millions and millions of people. Though the religions talk about peace on earth, they have all, except perhaps Buddhism and Hinduism, killed people. There is competition, aggression, each one seeking his own success, his own fulfilment. Externally we are in conflict and also inwardly. That's a fact; it is not a theory.

We have never inquired whether we can possibly be free from conflict. Inevitably, naturally, you will ask the speaker, 'Are *you* free from conflict?' If he were not, he wouldn't talk about it. That would be hypocrisy, and the speaker has practically all his life abhorred any kind of dishonest, hypocritical thinking or way of life. Now, to inquire into it together requires that you share, involve, commit yourself to find out whether conflict can end, while living in this world, not going off to some monastery or escaping into some ashram and all that silly nonsense. Why are we in conflict? What's the cause, the very nature, and structure of conflict? Most of us wait for an answer, for somebody to tell us. That's the function of the specialist. But there are no specialists here. We are asking each other, what is the cause of it, of wars, economic wars, social wars, and the destruction of human beings? What is the cause of it? Is it not nationalities, each nation thinking it is separate from the rest of the world? Not just nationalism, glorified tribalism, but also the ideologies of the totalitarian states and the democratic world, different beliefs, dialectical materialism on one side and belief in God, democratic ideals, on the other. They are still ideals. So ideals are at war; beliefs are at war. If you believe in certain forms of Christian dogmatism or the superstitions and dogmatism of Hinduism or Buddhism, these very beliefs, these very faiths, divide human beings. You are Catholic, Protestant, and there are countless divisions of Protestantism, as there are of Hinduism and Buddhism—there are North Buddhists and South Buddhists.

So the major cause of external conflict is division. Where there is division, there must be conflict; and in ourselves we are broken up, fragmented. Each one of us thinks he is separate from another—don't we? Religions throughout the world have encouraged the belief that you are separate, have a separate soul, separate individuality. Please don't reject this. We are not asking you to accept anything; we are inquiring.

In the Asiatic world, in India, they believe in this separate individuality, separate atman, as you do here in the Christian world —your soul is separate, to be saved. So from childhood this sense of division, of fragmentation within ourselves, is the basic cause of conflict, each one seeking his own salvation religiously—whatever that may mean. Each one wanting to express, fulfil himself, pursue his own ideals, own ambitions; and wife and husband do exactly the same thing, each one pursuing his own pleasure, own desire.

We can see that conflict must exist as long as there is division. Can this division end? Can this division, which has brought about such misery, confusion, ugliness, and brutality in the world, end in each one of us? You may ask this question intellectually and speculate about it. Perhaps some of you will say, 'No, it is not possible. In nature there is conflict. Everything is struggling to reach the light, bigger animals killing the smaller, and so on. As we are part of nature, we must live in conflict. That is how life is.' We have accepted this, not only as a tradition, but we have been encouraged, instructed, educated, to carry on with conflict.

Can this division in ourselves end? That is, the opposing desires, wanting, not wanting—you know, all the opposing energies that bring about such extraordinary conflict and misery—can all that end? It cannot possibly end through volition, that is, by will. Any form of volition, desire, motivation, wanting to end this conflict, that very desire to end conflict breeds further conflict. Doesn't it? I want to end conflict. Why? Because I hope to live a very peaceful life, and yet I have to live in this world—the world of business, science, relationship with each other, and so on, the modern world. Can I exist in this modern world without conflict? All the business world is based on conflict, competition, one firm against another. This is the endless conflict going on outwardly. And can the inward conflict end first? We are always asking about living in the external world without conflict, but we will find the right answer, right action, when we inquire into the conflict that each one of us has within. Can this division, opposing desires, opposing demands, individual urges, can all that division end?

It can only end if one can observe conflict, not try to end it or transform it into another form of conflict, but observe it. Which means to be aware, to give our complete attention to what conflict is and how it arises, the dualistic opposing drives of energy, just to observe it.

Have we ever observed anything completely? When you look at the sea, turbulent one morning and utterly quiet in the evening, have you ever observed wordlessly, without saying, how beautiful, how noisy, how disturbing it is? Have you ever observed with all your senses, with all your being, those extraordinary waters? To observe the sea without any reaction, just to watch. If you have ever done it, in the same way to observe conflict without any reaction, any motive, because the moment you have a motive that motive gives a direction. In that direction there is conflict, but just to observe the whole phenomenon of conflict, its cause, not only division, but imitation, conformity, all that. Just to be aware of the total nature and structure of conflict. When you give such complete attention, you will see for yourself whether conflict ends or not. But that requires, as we said, a great deal of energy, and that can come only when there is passion behind it, when you really want to find out. You give a great deal of time and energy to making money, as you do to being entertained. But you never give energy deeply and profoundly, in complete attention, to find out whether conflict can ever end.

So observation, not volition, not the action of will or resolution, but observing with all your being the nature and structure of conflict. Then one of the conditionings of the brain comes to an end. Because all human beings throughout the world are conditioned—as Catholics, Protestants, Hindus, Buddhists, Moslems, all the varieties of human invention.

We need to inquire into our conditioning: we are conditioned; you are Americans, following the American way of life. If you are Catholic, you have been conditioned for two thousand years; if you are Protestant, from the period of Henry VIII, who wanted to get rid of the pope in order to marry somebody or other. There are various forms of religious, social, cultural conditioning in India, Japan, and all the rest of the world. We are conditioned. And that conditioning is our consciousness.

We are conditioned by the newspapers, the media. This conditioning is our consciousness, not only biological reactions, sensory reactions, sexual reactions—that is part of our conditioning—but also we are conditioned by various forms of belief, faith, and dogma, by ideology, the various religious rituals. There is the question of linguistic conditioning, whether language conditions the brain.

So we are conditioned. Our consciousness is all the knowledge we have acquired, the experience, not only faith, belief, dogma, the rituals, but also fear, pleasure, sorrow, pain. Our conditioning is essentially knowledge. We have acquired knowledge for forty thousand years or more. And we are adding to that knowledge. The scientists are adding to knowledge day after day, month after month, to what they already know. And this knowledge is acquired through experience, testing, experimenting; if it doesn't succeed, they put it aside and begin again. There is this constant expansion of knowledge, both in ourselves and externally. And knowledge, because it is based on experience, is limited. There can be no complete knowledge about anything, including God. Knowledge is always, now and in the future, limited; it can be expanded, added to, but it still has its limitation.

So thought, which is born of knowledge, stored in the brain as memory, that thought is limited. There is no complete thought. Please, question this, doubt it, find out. This is very important because our consciousness is essentially thought, essentially knowledge. Our consciousness, the whole capacity of the brain, is therefore always limited, conditioned. Thought can imagine, speculate about, the immeasurable, endless space and so on, but whatever thought does, it is still limited. Do we see this fact? Because it is very important to understand this not merely intellectually but actually to see that whatever we are thinking, it is always limited, whether it is political, economic, or religious. Thought has invented God—sorry, I hope you will not be shocked by this. Just a minute. If you have no fear, absolutely no fear either of external incidents, accidents or inwardly, absolutely no fear of death, of tomorrow, of time, then what is the necessity for God? Then there is that state that is eternal—which we won't go into now.

So it is important, essential, that we understand the nature of thought. Thought has created the most astonishingly beautiful things—great paintings, great poems; thought has also created the whole world of technology, from the neutron bomb to instant communication, all the instruments of war, the submarine, the computer, and so on. Thought has done all this. The most beautiful cathedrals of Europe, and all the things that are in the cathedrals and in the churches, are put together by thought. But thought is, whatever it has created externally or inwardly, limited and therefore fragmented.

Thought is a material process; therefore nothing sacred is created by thought. Everything we call religion has been created by thought. You might say it is divine revelation straight from heaven, but that very idea 'straight from heaven' or 'revelation' is still the activity of thought, 'superconsciousness' and so on, all those inventions of the gurus that have come to this country, unfortunately. You have your own gurus, the priests; don't add any more. You have enough of them.

So we have to really understand the nature of thought. Thought is born of knowledge, stored in the brain as memory; so it's a material process. Knowledge is of course necessary at a certain level of existence—I need knowledge to write a letter, to go from here to there. Knowledge is necessary to drive a car, to do anything physically. Knowledge has a certain place. But we are asking: has knowledge any place in the psychological world? Has knowledge any place between you and your wife or husband? Knowledge being the memories that you have accumulated in that relationship, between man and woman, whether sexual memories, pleasure, pain, antagonism, and also the images, the knowledge, the pictures about each other.

So we are asking a very fundamental question: whether knowledge in relationship is not one of the factors of conflict. You certainly have, haven't you, an image about your wife—and the wife about the husband, or the girl about the boy, and so on. Each one creates not only his own image but also the image of another. You have certainly created one about the speaker, I am sure; otherwise you wouldn't be here. And that image is preventing you from actually understanding each other.

When one is living very intimately with another, you accumulate through that relationship, day in and day out, memories of each other. These memories, which are images, prevent actual relationship. This is a fact. These memories are the dividing factor and therefore cause conflict between man and woman. So can the recording processes of the brain in relationship stop? If one is married—suppose I am married, I am not, but suppose I am married. Don't ask me, 'Why are you not married?' That would be an easy way to dodge the issue. Suppose I am married: there is attraction, sex, and all the rest of it. Day after day, month after month, for years, I have put together a great deal of knowledge about her. She has done exactly the same thing about me. And these images, this knowledge that one has of each other, bring about a division and therefore conflict. Can this conflict in relationship end? Now that is most important, essential. If you can have it without a single shadow of conflict, relationship is one of the most wonderful things, and one cannot live on this marvellous earth without relationship.

Loneliness is a form of total separation, total division. Being frightened of loneliness, with all its depression, its ugliness, we try consciously or unconsciously to establish a relationship with another. We therefore become attached to the picture, the memory of the woman or the man, or whoever the person is. And real freedom is to be free from the image-building process; that is real freedom—not to do what you like, which is too childish, too utterly immature, but freedom that comes totally when in relationship there is no accumulation of memories. Is that possible? Or is it a vain hope, something to be desired in heaven, which is absurd, of course?

Let's inquire into it. The speaker has gone into it very deeply for himself, but to go into it *you* must inquire why the brain records. The brain records, that's part of its function, recording how to learn French or Russian, recording various business activities; the whole machinery of the brain is recording. But why should it record in relationship? Why should my brain record the insult or encouragement or flattery of my wife? Why should it? Have you ever inquired into it? Probably not. Probably it is too boring. Most of us are satisfied with the way we live—accepting, carrying on until we get old and die. To carry on that way is a waste of energy. There is no art, no beauty in that. Just carrying on, day after day, following the same routine, misery, confusion, insecurity, and at the end of it all, so meaninglessly, to die.

It is necessary for the brain to record at a certain level, physically: how to drive a car, how to be a good carpenter or some kind of ugly politician. But in relationship with each other, why should there be recording at all? Does that recording give us security in our relationship? Is there security in relationship? I believe there are more divorces in this country than marriages.

Relationship is a very, very serious matter. But the quality of that relationship is destroyed when the brain is recording all the petty little incidents, nagging, pleasures. You know what goes on in ordinary relationships, each one pursuing his own ambition, fulfilment, pleasure. That utterly destroys relationship.

Also, is love a matter of thought? Is love desire? Is love pleasure? Is love memory? Please do inquire into all this—not only intellectually but actually so that the very inquiry is action. When you act, that action demands passion, not just intellectual concept or desire. Love is not lust, love is not within the orbit of thought, and when the brain is merely a recording machine in a relationship, you destroy everything that is love.

You may say, it is very easy for you to talk that way because you are not married. Many people have told me this—which is nonsense. The speaker lives with a great many people, in India, Europe, and America, a great many, constantly. When the nature, structure, activity, and limitation of thought have really been understood, which means observed, that very observation is action. Then there is a totally different quality of relationship, because love is outside the brain, not within the confines of thought.

So our conditioning is, like fear, the movement of thought. We have lived with fear for thousands of years, and we are still afraid, outwardly and inwardly. Outwardly we want physical security. One must have physical security. But that outward security becomes insecurity when one seeks psychological security. We want psychological security first; psychologically to be safe, we want in our relationship to be completely secure—my permanent wife! Or if permanency doesn't exist with that woman, I will try and find it with another one. You may laugh, but this is what is happening in the world. Probably this is what has happened to you. Perhaps that is why you laugh it off so quickly.

One has to inquire very deeply whether there is any inward security, permanency in life. Or is the search for inward security, which is ultimately God, illusory, and therefore there is no security, psychologically, but only that supreme intelligence—not of books, not of knowledge—that comes, exists, only where there is love and compassion. That intelligence then acts. You may say, 'All this is so far-fetched, so complicated', but it isn't. Life—living—is a very complex process. You must know that much better than the speaker does. Getting to the office, the factory—our whole way of living is a very complex process. And that which is complex must be approached with great simplicity. To be psychologically simple, not stupidly simple, but to see the quality of simplicity. The word *innocence* means, etymologically, not to hurt and not to be hurt. But we are hurt from childhood by parents, by fellow students, through university, and so on; we are perpetually being wounded psychologically. That hurt we carry through life, with all its agony. When one is hurt, there is always the fear of being hurt again, so one builds a wall around oneself and resists. But never to be hurt is simplicity.

Now with that simplicity to approach the very complex problem of life, which is the art of living. All this requires a great deal of energy, passion, and a great sense of freedom to observe.

Rajghat, 12 November 1984

WOULD YOU LIKE to discuss why human beings live perpetually in conflict, have problems perpetually? Have you gone into it? Your lives are in conflict, aren't they? Be honest and simple for once. What is conflict? Opposing desires, opposing demands, opposing opinions: I think this, and you think that; my prejudice against your prejudice; my tradition against your tradition; my meditation against yours; my guru is better than your guru; deeper still, my selfishness against your selfishness. So there is this contradictory process going on in us, which is the dualistic attitude towards life. The good and the bad. Have you ever inquired whether there is a relationship between the good and the bad? Is this all something new? That is duality, you understand, hate and not hate.

Let's take one thing: violence and non-violence. Is there a relationship between violence and a brain that has no violence? If there is, then that implies a connection between the two. If there is a relationship between violence and that which is not violence—then one is born out of the other. Give your mind to this for a while. Two opposites: violence or, if you don't like violence, envy and not envy. If envy has a relationship with non-envy, then one is born out of the other.

Look, if love is related to hate or to jealousy—that is better—let's take a very ordinary daily fact. If love is related to hate, then it is not love, is it?

If that which is not violent is related to violence, it is still part of violence. So violence is something entirely different from that which is non-violence. If you see that fact, then conflict ceases. Look, if I am blind, I accept it. I can't keep struggling, saying I must have more light, I must see. I am blind. But if I don't accept it and say I must see, I must see, I must see, then there is conflict. This is a very simple fact. I accept I am blind. With the acceptance of the fact of blindness I have to cultivate different senses. I can feel how closely I come to a wall. Seeing the fact that I am blind has its own responsibility. But if I say constantly to myself I must see, I must see, I am in conflict.

This is what you are doing. If I accept that I am dull, I do so because I compare myself with you, who are clever. I know dullness only through comparison. I see you, very bright, very clever, intelligent—and I say, compared to her how dull I am. But if I don't compare, *I am what I am*. Right? I can then begin from there; but if I am comparing myself all the time with you, who are bright, intelligent, nice looking, capable, and all the rest of it, I am in perpetual conflict with you. But if I accept what I am—I am this—from there I can begin. So conflict exists only when we deny the actual fact of 'what is'. I am *this*, but if I am trying all the time to become *that*, I am in conflict. You are like that because you all engage in psychological becoming. You all want to become businessmen, holy, or meditate properly, don't you? So there is conflict. Instead of realizing the fact that I am violent and not moving away from that fact, I pretend not to be violent; and when I pretend not to be violent, conflict begins. So will you stop pretending and say, I am violent, let's deal with violence? When you have a toothache, you go to a dentist, you do something about it, but when you *pretend* you have no toothache . . . ! So conflict ends when you see things as they are and do not pretend something that is not.

Bombay, 7 February 1985

CAN YOU LOOK at something without the word? Can you look, as you are sitting here, at this person without the word, image, reputation, all that nonsense? Can you look at him? Is not the word the observer? Is not the word, the image, the memory, all that, the observer? Is not the observer the background of being a Hindu, or a Moslem, or whatever, with all the superstitions, the beliefs, the implications? It is memory that makes the observer seem different from the thing observed. Can you look, observe, without the background, the past memories impinging upon the thing being observed? When you do that, there is only that which is being observed. There is no observer observing the thing observed.

When there is a difference, a division, between the observer or the one who witnesses, between the observer and the observed, there must—as we said before—be conflict. And to understand why human beings live in conflict from the moment they are born till they die is to find out why this division between the observer and the observed exists, or whether there is only the thing observed.

What we are saying is, wherever there is a division, there must be conflict. That's a law, an eternal law. Where there is separation, a division, a breaking up into two parts, there must be conflict. That conflict ultimately becomes war, killing people. As is being shown now in the world, in America, Russia, Lebanon, the

Islamic world, and the non-Islamic world, there is conflict. So to understand and be free of conflict, really be free of it, is to understand why the observer becomes so dominant, separate from him, or her, the person or thing being observed. When I observe, if I am married or have a girlfriend, there is a division between us, an actual, not only physical, division but a traditional division, the authority of the parent, the authority of someone, so there is always division in our relationships and always therefore conflict between human beings.

There are very few human beings in the world who have a relationship in which conflict doesn't exist, and that conflict exists because we have separated the observer from the observed. I am different from my anger, my envy, my sorrow; therefore being different, there is conflict. That is, 'I must get rid of sorrow. Tell me how to overcome sorrow. Tell me what to do with my fear.' So there is conflict, all the time. But you *are* sorrow. You are not different from sorrow, from anger, from your sexual desires, are you? You are not different from the loneliness you feel—you are lonely. But we say, 'Yes, I'm lonely, but I must escape from it'. So I go to the temple or some entertainment. You are not different from the quality of which you are; that quality *is* you. I *am* anger, sorrow, loneliness, depression. Now, before, when I separated, I acted upon my sorrow. If I was lonely, I escaped from loneliness, tried to overcome or analyse or fill it with all kinds of amusement or religious activity. But if I am lonely, I can't do anything about it. I am lonely—but not I am lonely as something different from me—I am that. Before I acted upon it; now I can't act upon it because I *am* that.

So what happens when the observer is the observed? When the anger *is* me, then what takes place? Have you inquired into this, or do you just say, 'Yes, I am the observer and the observed'? That is meaningless. But go into it and find out if anger is ever different from you. The tradition, the conditioning, says, 'I am different from my anger', and therefore you acted upon it. But when you realize that you are anger, what do you do, what happens?

First, all conflict ceases. All conflict ceases when you realize that you are that. I am brown—finished. It's a fact—light
brown or dark brown or purple or whatever colour it is. So you
eliminate altogether this divisive process that brings conflict in
yourself.

Also, why is it that we make an abstraction from a fact?
The fact is I am anger, I am jealous, I am lonely. Why do we make
that into an idea, an abstraction? Is it easier to make an abstraction
than to face the fact? Because I can play with ideas. I say, 'Yes, this
is a good idea; that is a bad idea; convince me; you don't convince
me'. I can go on like that. When there is no abstraction but only
the fact, then I have to deal with it. But then I separate myself
and say, 'I am going to do something about it'. When one realizes
there is no separation—you are that, you are 'what is', you are a
Hindu, a Moslem, a Christian; you are a businessman, you are
ugly, you are brutal; you are all that—then you have eliminated altogether the sense of division in yourself, and therefore conflict
ends. Do you know what the brain is like when there is no conflict? When the brain is in perpetual conflict, as most people's
brains are, what happens to that brain? It's wounded, hurt.

Probably you have lived so long with conflict, pain, sorrow, and fear, and you've said, 'It's part of my life. I'll accept it',
and you've gone on that way. You've never inquired what conflict
does to the brain, the psyche, of a human being. If one is constantly beaten, bombarded with conflict, do you know what happens to the brain? It shrinks. It becomes very small, limited, ugly.
That's what is happening to all of us. So the fairly intelligent man
asks, 'Why should I live in conflict for the rest of my life?' He begins to inquire what conflict is. Conflict must exist where there is
division—inside as well as outside. This division, deeply, fundamentally, is between the 'me', the observer, and the thing observed. Two separate activities going on—which is not true,
because you are anger, you are violence. If you come to that point
and realize that the observer is the observed, there is activity that
is totally different.

From Krishnamurti's Notebook, *31 September 1961*

THE SUN WAS setting in great clouds of colour behind the Roman hills; they were brilliant, splashed across the sky, and the whole earth was made splendid, even the telegraph poles and the endless rows of buildings. It was soon becoming dark, and the car was going fast. The hills faded, and the country became flat. To look with thought and to look without thought are two different things. To look at those trees by the roadside and the buildings across the dry fields with thought keeps the brain tied to its own moorings of time, experience, memory; the machinery of thought is working endlessly, without rest, without freshness; the brain is made dull, insensitive, without the power of recuperation. It is everlastingly responding to challenge, and its response is inadequate and not fresh. To look with thought keeps the brain in the groove of habit and recognition; it becomes tired and sluggish; it lives within the narrow limitations of its own making. It is never free. This freedom takes place when thought is not looking; to look without thought does not mean a blank observation, absence in distraction.

When thought does not look, then there is only observation, without the mechanical process of recognition and comparison, justification and condemnation; this seeing does not fatigue the brain, for all mechanical processes of time have stopped. Through complete rest the brain is made fresh, to respond without reaction, to live without deterioration, to die without the torture of problems. To look without thought is to see without the interference of time, knowledge, and conflict. This freedom to see is not a reaction; all reactions have causes; to look without reaction is not indifference, aloofness, a cold-blooded withdrawal. To see without the mechanism of thought is total seeing, without particularization and division, which does not mean that there are not separation and dissimilarity. The tree does not become a house or the house a tree. Seeing without thought does not put the brain to sleep; on the contrary, it is fully awake, attentive, without friction and pain. Attention without the borders of time is the flowering of meditation.

Sources and Acknowledgments

From the report of the first public talk at Ojai, 27 May 1945, in volume IV of *The Collected Works of J. Krishnamurti*, copyright © 1991 Krishnamurti Foundation of America.

From the report of the fourth public talk at Ojai, 17 June 1945, in volume IV of *The Collected Works of J. Krishnamurti*, copyright © 1991 Krishnamurti Foundation of America.

From the report of the eighth public talk in Bombay, 7 March 1948, in volume IV of *The Collected Works of J. Krishnamurti*, copyright © 1991 Krishnamurti Foundation of America.

From the report of the second public talk in Bangalore, 11 July 1948, in volume V of *The Collected Works of J. Krishnamurti*, copyright © 1991 Krishnamurti Foundation of America.

From the report of the first public talk in Poona, 1 September 1948, in volume V of *The Collected Works of J. Krishnamurti*, copyright © 1991 Krishnamurti Foundation of America.

From the report of the second public talk in Bombay, 19 February 1950, in volume VI of *The Collected Works of J. Krishnamurti*, copyright © 1991 Krishnamurti Foundation of America.

From the report of the fifteenth talk to students at Rajghat School, Varanasi, 22 January 1954, in volume VIII of *The Collected Works of J. Krishnamurti*, copyright © 1991 Krishnamurti Foundation of America.

From the report of the first public talk at Rajghat, 9 January 1955, in volume VIII of *The Collected Works of J. Krishnamurti*, copyright © 1991 Krishnamurti Foundation of America.

From the report of the first public talk at Ojai, 6 August 1955, in volume IX of *The Collected Works of J. Krishnamurti*, copyright © 1991 Krishnamurti Foundation of America.